Donald A. Foster.

From Mother & Father.

6 December, 1928.

RELIGIOUS THOUGHT IN THE
OXFORD MOVEMENT

RELIGIOUS THOUGHT
IN THE
OXFORD MOVEMENT

BY

C. C. J. WEBB, M.A., F.B.A.

ORIEL PROFESSOR OF THE PHILOSOPHY OF THE CHRISTIAN
RELIGION IN THE UNIVERSITY OF OXFORD

LONDON

SOCIETY FOR PROMOTING
CHRISTIAN KNOWLEDGE

NEW YORK AND TORONTO : THE MACMILLAN CO.

1928

Printed in Great Britain

PREFACE

THE following chapters contain the substance of a course of lectures delivered by me in 1925 as Oriel Professor of the Philosophy of the Christian Religion. I have thought that it might be of interest, now that the centenary of the Oxford Movement is near at hand—indeed, if the publication of Keble's *Christian Year* rather than the delivery of his Assize Sermon, which Newman reckoned as the birthday of the Movement, be taken as the date, has already passed—to review the philosophical principles which seem to have underlain the religious teaching of the Tractarian divines. That teaching has had an effect upon the theology and religion of their country and of the Christian world sufficiently important to justify such a survey as I have endeavoured to make in these pages ; a survey which, however, does not pretend to do more than indicate certain leading features of a body of thought which deserves, and will no doubt some day receive, a far more thorough and extensive treatment.

OXFORD, 1927.

CONTENTS

RELIGIOUS THOUGHT IN THE OXFORD MOVEMENT

I

INTRODUCTORY

§ 1. THE SUBJECT PROPOSED

THE student of the life of modern England will
have to recognize that in many ways the Movement which (though neither the first nor the last
of movements affecting the religious life of this
country with a claim to be so called) has by
general consent appropriated to itself the name
of the Oxford Movement was one of very considerable importance. While its doctrinal teaching probably affected the religion of the nation
as a whole less than is often supposed, it unquestionably created a new ideal of the Church's
ministry and a new type of clergyman ; and its
influence in this respect has spread not only
far beyond the boundaries of the party in the
Anglican Communion which would recognize
itself or be recognized by others as the heir of
the Tractarian tradition ; it has extended outside
the limits of the Anglican Communion itself. It

has, moreover, as a consequence of this, trans-
formed the idea in the popular mind of what the
externals, at any rate, of worship are and should
be ; and those who now dislike the changes introduced by those who go by the name—preferred
for themselves by the men of the Oxford Movement—of Anglo-Catholics would often be sur-
prised to know to how great an extent the fashions
to which they cling are themselves the creation
of that Movement in its earlier phases.

Moreover, the influence of the Oxford Movement can be traced in a wider field than any which
can be called ecclesiastical. It unquestionably
made a contribution by no means negligible to
the movement for the emancipation of the women
of the middle class from the restrictions imposed
upon them by the social customs of a hundred
years ago. And very likely there might be found
other instances in which the social development
of that stratum of society which the Movement
chiefly affected owes not a little to the impact of
its ideals upon the mind of the generation which
grew to manhood or womanhood in the fifth,
sixth, seventh, and eighth decades of last
century. But it is not with this aspect of the
Oxford Movement that I am proposing to deal.
Nor do I ask my readers to concentrate their
attention upon the greatest figure in the Movement, that of John Henry Newman. The charm
of his style, the fascination of his personality,
the independence of his ideas, the elusiveness of

his point of view, notwithstanding that he is for ever, as it were, inviting his hearers and readers to assist at the drama, so absorbing to himself, of his own feelings and thoughts, an elusiveness which suggests the title of M. Bremond's book, *Le Mystère de Newman;* all this has naturally created a Newman literature, which is not likely to be even yet complete, and which would afford material for an interesting survey. But Newman, though the greatest figure in the Movement, is not the Movement, nor is he even typical of it ; it cannot indeed be understood apart from him, but he is at once more and less than it. There are aspects of it which, though he may sometimes have given them expression in haunting language, were never really congenial to his mood ; and his secession to Rome revealed a real diversity between his mind and that of his colleagues who remained in the Church of their baptism. On the other hand, he was unquestionably the man of greatest genius among its leaders ; and there is much in him which is essentially his, but is not characteristic of the Movement to which his extraordinary gifts gave so great an impetus, and over which they have cast so enduring a glamour.

Lastly, I do not intend to discuss the influence of the Oxford Movement on ecclesiastical theory. Obviously it was concerned to insist upon the importance of ecclesiastical order in general, and upon a certain conception of what is essential to such order in particular ; and the whole interest of the most arresting and dramatic chapters in the history of its leaders centres about their satisfaction or dissatisfaction with this particular conception ; it was, moreover, in the main, agreement or disagreement therewith that determined the attitude of its contemporaries towards it. Moreover, it is clear that much might be said of the positions in dogmatic theology taken up by the teachers of the Movement ; and I should certainly not deny that the expression '' religious thought '' could be rightly applied to these. But my purpose is to discover the contribution, if any, which the Movement we are considering made to what may be called the Philosophy of Religion, a subject which will, however, often trench upon that of dogmatic theology, between which and philosophy of religion no rigid line can, in my opinion, be drawn. The distinction between them is rather one of the angle from which they are respectively approached than in their subject-matter. In the one the starting-point is the teaching of Scripture and of ecclesiastical tradition ; in the other the problems raised or suggested by religious experience as to the general nature of reality. But the true significance of dogmatic theology is not to be understood apart from its philosophical implications ; nor is the student of the philosophy of religion justified in ignoring the record of religious experience preserved in the dogmatic formulation which has approved itself to the community that has mediated this religious experience to the individuals who are its subjects.

§ 2. THEOLOGICAL ATMOSPHERE OF THE OXFORD MOVEMENT

In a series of lectures which I have printed along with others in a book published in 1923, and called, from the subject of those lectures, *A Century of Anglican Theology,*[1] I connected the Oxford Movement and the school of thought which created it with the general movement of thought in Europe, illustrated in philosophy and literature by such names as those of Goethe and Hegel, which corresponded in the intellectual realm to the restoration of the political and social edifice after its ruin in the great Revolution begun in France in the last years of the eighteenth century ; while as the spiritual analogue of that Revolution itself I pointed to the philosophy of Kant, which the poet Heine has, in a striking chapter of his *Deutschland,*[2] presented in this very capacity. As I connected the Oxford Movement and its congeners elsewhere—for it was not the only movement of the time, as Newman himself recognized, to press upon the conscience a new emphasis upon the conception of the Church and upon the claims of the historic tradition embodied therein—with the reaction in European philosophy from Kant's attitude of rationalistic criti-

[1] By Mr. Basil Blackwell.   [2] Buch III.

cism and the construction of an idealistic theory of the universe which would justify the revolt of the Romantic Movement against the limitations imposed upon the mind by the prosaic common sense of the preceding period; so I suggested a correspondence between the subjectivism and individualism of Kant's own philosophy and the similar characteristics of such religious movements as that known in Germany by the name of Pietism, and that which in England we designate as Evangelicalism.

But whatever measure of truth there may be—and much there no doubt is—in this alignment, the world of thought is not so neatly mapped out, nor are its compartments cut off so sharply from one another, that one can expect to find the indication of this kind of correspondence yield a sufficient account of the movements in which it may be observed. It will be one of the things to which I desire to call your attention in the present course of lectures that the thought which lay at the heart of the Oxford Movement bears in certain important respects a striking resemblance to the ethical doctrine of Kant, but is distinguished from it by its combination in the minds of its exponents with elements of a quite different kind, closely akin to some which we find in the post-Kantian philosophy, and which form the point of contact between the Oxford Movement and the general European tendency which it is the custom to call Romantic.

I do not suppose—quite the contrary—that this coincidence of the theory underlying the teaching of the Oxford divines with that embodied in Kant's moral philosophy was due to a conscious submission of those divines to Kant's influence. It is nowhere more plain than in Newman's own teaching; but Newman in his Oxford days probably knew little or nothing of Kant and, I believe, never actually read him till 1884, when he was eighty-three and a Cardinal—only three years, as I am amused to recollect, before I myself, as an undergraduate of twenty-two, found in the Kantian treatise on the *Fundamental Principles of the Metaphysic of Morals* a book which made, I suppose, a greater impression upon me than any other single work that ever fell in my way. It is, of course, not to be forgotten that the influence of such a thinker as Kant on the minds of educated men fifty years later is not confined to those who have actually studied him, or even to those who know that he is the original source of thoughts which they have unconsciously imbibed with the spiritual atmosphere they have breathed; and in this particular case the influence of Kant upon Coleridge, and through him upon Wordsworth, is undoubted, and so, too, is that of both these on the men of the Oxford Movement, Newman among the rest. But while this is to be borne in mind, it would, I am sure, be a mistake to attribute much to direct, or even to indirect, Kantian influence in the matter. The "moralism'' which, as Dr. Brilioth in his recent very interesting book on the Oxford Movement called *The Anglican Revival*[1] has justly observed, is characteristic of Anglican and, one may say, of English thought, and this, together with a no less characteristically English aversion from abstract thought, affords a sufficiently relevant origin for a view which, in its emphasis upon morality as the root of religion and in its accompanying revulsion from merely rationalistic proofs of divine government, reminds us of Kant's doctrine of the primacy of the practical reason, and of the postulation by this same ''practical reason'' of God and immortality as the primary and only dependable argument for the existence of either. The parallel is none the less worth calling attention to and none the less worth the trouble of elaborating.

§ 3. THE OXFORD MOVEMENT AND EVOLUTION

But before I elaborate it, it will, I think, be convenient to indicate certain facts about the intellectual atmosphere of the Oxford Movement which we must bear in mind in our examination of its teaching. It is not yet a century—though it is only five years short of a century—since the day which Newman reckoned as the birthday of the Movement,[2] that on which Keble preached

[1] Longmans, 1925.   [2] *Apologia,* ed. 1864, p. 100.

16

his University Sermon on *National Apostasy;* yet there are at least two factors in the intellectual environment of the educated theologian to-day which make the position of his predecessor at that time seem strangely remote. One is the principle of Evolution; the other is modern biblical criticism.

The principle of development had been made central in philosophy by Hegel a few years before the time of which we were speaking; but Hegel was scarcely known at all in England, and it was only after the publication of Darwin's *Origin of Species* thirty years later and the ambitious attempt of Herbert Spencer to provide an account of the universe based upon evolution as he understood it—however unphilosophically unsatisfactory that attempt may have been—that this principle became part of the general intellectual outfit of educated Englishmen. That the change of form which as undeniably takes place in the course of time in societies, institutions, creeds, as it does in the passage of an organism from its separation from the parent organism to its production of a similar distinct organism, must be regarded as belonging to the very essence of that which undergoes it, and not merely as the corruption or improvement of something which might have been as it was without change; this thought, so familiar to us, was, as a universal principle, strange even to many philosophers in the eighteenth and early nineteenth centuries. New-

17   B

man himself, as is well known, following in the steps of certain foreign Roman Catholic thinkers —de Maistre in France and Möhler in Germany —eventually worked out for himself a theory of Development in doctrine, to justify the acceptance of an institution so manifestly diverse, both in theory and practice, from the primitive Church as the Church of his own day, as being, notwithstanding this diversity, essentially identical with that primitive Church. But, as worked out by him, the theory, although we must give its author credit here as elsewhere for that kind of instinctive perception of the trend of thought which is a note of genius, yet bears all the marks of an opportunist creation. And its working out, we must remember, landed him outside the Anglican Church in the Church of Rome. The movement within the Anglican Church was therefore all the more likely to cling to the static or pre-evolutionary view of the Church with which that generation had started, that desertion of it had led its late leader to desert it also ; and, in point of fact, it was only the publication of *Lux Mundi* half a century later, and within my own recollection, that marked—though, of course, it did not initiate—the decisive adoption of the evolutionary principle as a ruling idea in theology by the party which inherited the tradition of the Tractarians. When we read the Tracts themselves and the other literature of the Oxford Movement, we are, we feel throughout, in an atmosphere profoundly different from our own, in the absence from it of that *assumption* of development or evolution as a universal *fact,* at least where there is anything we can call *life,* however we interpret it—and readers of Mr. Joseph's recent Herbert Spencer Lecture on the *Idea of Evolution*[1] will have learned thence, if they had not previously discovered, how difficult it is to know what precisely we *mean* by evolution—that *assumption* of it, I say, as a fact, which is to us as much a matter of course as our assumption of the earth's motion or even of the uniformity of Nature. In all these cases it is easier for most of us to make them than to justify our assumptions : in all we might even reserve the right to doubt or qualify them ; but still we make the assumptions and count upon others making them ; and, as our fathers did with the other scientific doctrine which I have mentioned, so we now do also with that of evolution, at least in the case of life and of whatever can in any sense be called living.

§ 4. THE OXFORD MOVEMENT AND BIBLICAL CRITICISM

This assumption, then, is one thing which is part of the very stuff of our thoughts as it was not of that of the Oxford divines ; and another change, of far less universal significance, but,

[1] Oxford, 1924.

where Christian theology is in question, of hardly less importance, is the acceptance of what is called the "higher criticism" of the Bible.

I say the acceptance. For, without in the least desiring to minimize the uncertainty of many results of that criticism, or to ignore the great diversity of opinion among scholars upon some of the most important questions to which it gives rise, I suppose that the recent proceedings in Tennessee have made us here all feel how remote the whole attitude of the most conservative scholar or student among ourselves is from that of the "Fundamentalists," to whom the Bible, just as it stands, is the verbally exact communication by supernatural authority of infallible and absolute knowledge. No doubt the leaders of the Tractarians were scholars, to whom the uncertainty due to the chances of textual transmission was perfectly familiar, and no doubt also they had reflected, as uneducated Fundamentalists have not, on the variety of ways, other than the relation of historic fact, in which the revelation of divine truth is possible. Moreover, as I shall afterwards have occasion in another connection to point out, it was a characteristic part of their message to urge the precedence of certain parts of the Bible over others, of the New Testament over the Old, of the Gospels, as recording the actual words and deeds of God manifest in the flesh, even over the inspired commentary upon these in the Epistles. Nor need we forget that

Newman in particular had, as he remarks himself,[1] freer views on Biblical criticism than others
of his party, learned from the conversation of
Blanco White. But when all is said and done, the
whole attitude towards the Bible which it was
natural to the Tractarians to adopt was different
from that which any scholar of the present
generation is expected to adopt. Perhaps I may
put the matter thus : Then—and, indeed, much
later (we may see this occasionally implied even
in the work of so famous a figure in the history
of New Testament criticism as Westcott) it was
taken for granted that because something was
found within the covers of the Bible it must teach
some important lesson, if not in its primary or
literal sense, then in another, a "mystical" or
"allegorical" sense ; and, conversely, it was no
less felt that, if something was put forward as a
religious duty or as the truth about a matter per-
taining to religion, there was something lacking
to its force until a text could be found which,
somehow interpreted, would provide it with the
necessary scriptural sanction.

Now, I do not say that the assumptions and
the feeling which I have described are not still
active in the minds of those who were, like myself, brought up at a time before the Churches had
opened their doors as widely as they now have
done to critical inquiry, or of those who, though
younger themselves, having been educated under

[1] *Apol.*, p. 65.

the influence of an earlier generation, have not been brought into contact with the critical inquiries which make up so much of the theological training given in a University at the present day. Nevertheless, I think I may affirm that there are scholars, even orthodox and conservative scholars, younger than myself, who scarcely realize what a view of the Bible was which was quite familiar to my own contemporaries and was almost universal among the professedly orthodox at the time of the Oxford Movement. I do not think that, before leaving this topic, it will be irrelevant to dwell a little longer upon it, and to distinguish, if I may, from the purely uncritical reverence for the letter of Scripture which I have been saying has, in scholarly circles, passed away, some (as it seems to me) quite reasonable attitudes which I would not be thought to confuse with this or to condemn as ignorant and obsolete.

I do not think it is possible for us to be content with the picture, which, perhaps, satisfied some of us once, of God as a kind of editor, who, selecting certain narratives, poems, codes, for admission into the body of inspired Scripture, put nothing in but what could yield spiritual profit, left nothing out but what was no necessary part of his message to man. This kind of view was itself, of course, what we may call a *mediating* view. It no longer regarded God as the immediate *Author* of every word in the Bible; he was rather, as I have said, its *Editor;* it was in the

selection of material rather than in its origination
that the action of the Divine Spirit was to be
traced. But, like most such mediating views, it
has lost something of the simplicity of the view
which it replaced, without really being adequate
to meet the demands to which it was conceded.
Few younger biblical critics but would, I think,
feel that the anthropomorphism involved in the
belief in a literal divine authorship is retained only
in a less dignified form by the conception of a
divine editorship. Nevertheless, while fully recognizing that in this, as in other cases, we "have
the treasure" of the divine revelation "in earthen
vessels,"[1] and that we need not hesitate to admit
the presence in the Bible of passages which came
there for reasons quite other than their spiritual
value, we may not unreasonably feel that the
fact that the Bible, as a whole, has actually been
found to be (as it has) the spiritual food of so
many generations of Christian people, warrants
us in doing two things. In the first place, it
warrants us in holding our hand as regards anything which is of the nature of spiritual teaching
(prophecy or poetry or reflection or story about
God, not, e.g., a catalogue of princes or cities
or a sanitary regulation) before we assume that it
does not contribute something toward that general
drift, that pervading mood, in virtue of which the
Bible has been the Word of God to thousands.
In the second place, we should be merely pedantic

[1] 2 Cor. iv. 7.

in refusing to avail ourselves of interpretations even of passages which *we* do not doubt to have been intended for quite other purposes than spiritual edification (such as the catalogues and regulations I instanced before) which the piety of ages that believed every part of Scripture to be inspired may have found in them. Many such interpretations may have become, fanciful as they seem to us as interpretations of those passages, part of our spiritual inheritance. It would be as unreasonable to refuse to refer to these (without pretending that we think that they give the original writer's meaning) as to refuse to draw inspiration from religious pictures and poems, the subjects of which we consider legendary. It is another matter *ourselves* to invent "mystical" interpretations, or to put up, as if they were representations of facts, representations of what we are assured are merely legends.

That may be very dangerous, playing fast and loose with our sense of truth. But it is otherwise with the interpretations devised of old by men who did it in good faith. The New Testament writers themselves, of course, often in that way turned to good purpose mistaken interpretations of the Old ; and so did the imagination of patriotic and medieval times. "They shall look on him whom they pierced." "God reigneth from the tree." Such texts are surely sacred in the sense which has been given them by tradition, though it be not that of the original writers. My Hebraist

friends tell me that "Verily thou art a God that
hidest thyself" does not mean what Pascal supposed : but the thought of the *Deus absconditus,*
though suggested by a misunderstanding of the
text, may, notwithstanding, mean a great deal
to us.

This open-eyed use of passages which happen
to be in the Bible, and therefore have been turned
by others who took their inspiration for granted to
purposes of edification which were not in the minds
of those who first wrote them, must not, then,
be confused with a belief, which a scholar could
now scarcely entertain without doing violence to
his mentality as a civilized man of the present
day, that everything within the covers of the
Bible is there because it is inspired. On the other
hand, we may say that what we are assured is
true and right does not gain a new sanction
because we can twist or even legitimately use
some biblical text to establish it, without saying
that it is no argument at all against a religious
view or moral requirement that it is not taught in
Scripture. It is certainly not a final argument,
nor even an argument at all against some
view or requirement clearly seen to be in harmony
with the general outlook for which the Bible, as
the sacred book of our religion, stands. But there
is a *prima facie* reason for further consideration of
any religious novelty in the fact that it is nowhere
suggested in this great and various body of literature, embodying the religious experience which we

count as central and normative. We are, I think, bound to ask ourselves whether this absence of it from the Bible may not be explained by some real incongruity of the view or precept in question with the spirit of our religion. But I would readily grant that the answer may sometimes be in the negative, as well as sometimes in the affirmative.

This subject has, perhaps, led us somewhat far aside from our main subject ; but not unprofitably, if it help us to a more definite conception of the theological atmosphere which the men of the Oxford Movement breathed, and which was so unlike our own, since it was the atmosphere of a world in which the idea of evolution was a stranger, and in which the beginnings of biblical criticism, as we understand the expression, were either unperceived or, if perceived, regarded with dread and suspicion, not only by those who were ready to sympathize with the Tractarians, but by those Evangelicals and old-fashioned Protestants with whom they had least in common.

II

THE "VIA MEDIA" OF ANGLICANISM

§ 1. ANGLICANISM AS A "VIA MEDIA"

A PHRASE which played a considerable part in
the theological controversy initiated by the
Oxford Movement was that of the *via media* used
to describe the historic position of the Anglican
Church. The claim was not a new one; it finds,
perhaps, its most striking expression in the well-
known lines of the typically Anglican poet,
George Herbert, in which, after describing the
Church of Rome as the painted lady on the hills,
and the Church reformed after the Genevan
model as the undrest lady in the valley,

> " So shy of dressing that her hair doth lie
>   About her ears,"

of whom it may be said that—

> " While she avoids her neighbour's pride
>   She wholly goes on the other side,
>   And nothing wears,"

he thus addresses the Church of England (which
he here calls, by the way, "the British
Church ") :

> " But, dearest Mother (what those miss),
>   The mean thy praise and glory is
>   And long may be !"

27

And it does in a very real sense indicate a characteristic of that Church which has been the source both of its peculiar strength and of its peculiar weakness.

The extremes between which the mean adopted by the Church of England lies are, of course, as organized institutions, the Church of Rome on the one side and the rest of the Churches which have accepted the Reformation on the other. The description of Herbert has in view, no doubt, especially those technically called "Reformed" along with the Puritans in his own country and time, who would have had the English doctrines and forms of worship conform more nearly than they did to those authorized by Calvin and his colleagues. The Lutheran Churches were less directly in his view, for their connection with and influence on the religious life of this country was, in his day, far less than that of the Churches whose spiritual metropolis was Geneva. But even the Lutheran Churches, though some of them had retained in some respects more of the outward ornaments of the medieval Church than the Anglican itself, and though some institutions of that Church were less completely in abeyance among them than in England, yet, representing as they did the first organized secession from the old Catholic unity, were more definitely and irretrievably ranged in the opposite camp to Rome, and, having (except, perhaps, indeed, in Sweden) broken the chain of the episcopal succession which still linked the Anglican ministry with that of the pre-Reformation Church, were not equally qualified to mediate between the two great branches of Western Christendom which are conveniently designated by the titles of Catholic and Protestant respectively.

§ 2. CATHOLICISM AND PROTESTANTISM

It will be, I think, useful if I now attempt very roughly and summarily to set forth some of the salient features in which Catholicism and Protestantism are contrasted, not so much in their formal theology (though this, of course, lies behind their more obvious differences) as in their general type of piety and conduct. I shall then point out in what principal respects the Anglican type of religion may be said to mediate between the two ; and this will form a natural introduction to a consideration of the principles of the Oxford Movement, a movement the essence of which consisted in a revival of attention to certain elements in the Anglican tradition, in virtue of which it was distinguished from the general tradition of Protestantism and approximated to the Catholic tradition, while at the same time claiming to retain others, in virtue of which the Church of England could not throw in its lot with the Roman Church as actually existing.

In the period in which the Middle Ages came to an end, the period of the double movement which we call in one aspect the Renaissance and in another the Reformation, the two sides of medieval life fall apart which had during the Middle Ages been held together in a unity by the international institutions which embodied the ideal of a culture at once classical and Christian. Such a culture in the period of the barbarian invasions of the Roman Empire had been received by the invading peoples, as it were, *en bloc,* on their conversion and civilization by the Roman Church, without discrimination between its classical and Christian factors. On the other hand, when the growing secularization of the Church, after the cessation of the persecutions and its establishment as the religion of the State, led to a reaction in the shape of an exaggerated asceticism, and the notion of a higher and a lower moral standard, of a technically "religious" life and a secular life which is yet permissible for Christians, obtained currency, a dualism arose which worked itself out in results leading at the time of the Reformation to a violent attempt to establish a single standard of Christian conduct, without any recognition of a technically "religious" life, transcending in merit that of the secular Christian who discharged his duties as a householder and citizen.

To begin with the process of the disruption of the medieval unity. This process was a complicated one, and one may recognize two controversies which crossed and recrossed each other. There was the controversy between the classical culture, now revealed through the recovery of the knowledge of Greek in the West as Hellenism, and the religious tradition of the Christian Church ; and there was the controversy between the international institutions which belonged to Christendom as a single community, a Church-Empire, and the national institutions which in the several countries of Western Europe had been, during the medieval period, advancing towards maturity within that single community. The local position in Italy of the Apostolic See of Rome, the religious centre of Western Christendom, led to consequences of vast historic importance. For it was in Italy that the scholars of the Greek Empire, flying before the armies of the Turk, first arrived with their treasure of Greek learning and letters ; and it aided their welcome there that Italy was itself one of the ancient homes of the classical culture, in which it had never become wholly extinct. The result was that, seated as it was in Italy, the Papacy—the greatest, and, now that the Empire as an international power was but a shadow of its past greatness, the most effective of the international institutions of the Middle Ages—was, as we may say, captured by Hellenism. Religious discontent with the neo-paganism which consequently became rampant in the historic centre of Christendom thus tended to ally itself with national aspirations against the pretensions of the Papacy to exploit the devotion of countries outside Italy in the interest of the

splendours of the art-loving and often irreligious
or even unbelieving Court of the Roman Pontiffs,
as when the proceeds of the sale of those in-
dulgences, the preaching of which in Germany
was the proximate cause of Luther's revolt, were
devoted to the building of the new St. Peter's ;
or as when, under the system by which the Pope
claimed the right to " provide " (as the technical
expression went) incumbents for all ecclesiastical
benefices, Italian kinsmen and favourites of the
Pope were quartered on the rich bishoprics,
dignitaries, and livings of countries with which
they had no connection and which they regarded
merely as sources of income. Hence we find the
religious Reformation readily taking the form of
insistence on the rights of national churches
against the Pope, and—as the only effective
means of securing these—on the rights of national
princes to govern the Church each in his own
dominions. It is well known how important a
doctrine of the English Reformation in particular
was that of the Royal Supremacy in matters
ecclesiastical. On the other hand, the national
sovereigns—and this, again, is especially exemplified in the history of England—utilized this
religious discontent as a weapon against the international claims of the Papacy, which, when
admitted, necessarily restricted their own
autonomy.

Passing from the side of this movement which
exhibits a disruption of the medieval unity to that

complementary aspect which exhibits an attempt to abolish the old moral dualism, there can, I think, be no reasonable doubt that the moral standard of the later Middle Ages was low and that the great religious revival of the thirteenth century, whose central figure was St. Francis of Assisi—than whom the Church can, perhaps, show no more striking example of Christian sanctity—did not in the long run succeed in removing this reproach. The Reformation on its moral side was a revolt against hypocrisy. This word had long been familiar—we find it so used, for example, in the *Policraticus* of John of Salisbury, written in the middle of the twelfth century and dedicated to the author's friend, Thomas Becket, whose shrine at Canterbury afterwards became the great object of English pilgrimage—as especially applicable to "religious" persons in the technical sense—monks, that is, and, later on, friars. For these, while pretending to a higher life than the secular Christian's, did often, in fact, lead a lower one ; one less industrious, because they had not the duties of bread-winners and citizens to perform ; in many cases more self-indulgent, where the wealth of the monastic foundations made easy and assured a comfortable life within the limits of a rule which was sometimes not very severe and had become habitual to those who had always been under it ; and often also less chaste, as was inevitably the case where marriage was impossible and great numbers of the monks and friars had adopted their profession not through any enthusiasm for a stricter life, but rather for a secure maintenance, much as a modern Frenchman becomes a *fonctionnaire* if he can. Of this last-mentioned fault the parochial clergy, upon whom celibacy was enforced, were also often accused in comparison with the married lay-folk ; though it was recognized that these " secular " clergy were, unlike the monks and friars, as much occupied as their neighbours, and for the most part no better off than they.

Thus the Reformation naturally involved the abolition of the religious Orders and the permission of marriage to the clergy. The unification of the moral standard appeared in the light of a moral reform. It is true that there was much loss as well as gain in the disappearance of institutions which afforded an opportunity for the growth of certain fine types of character in special cases which could hardly otherwise be secured ; although they had doubtless lent themselves also to certain kinds of scandalous "hypocrisy"— that is, discrepancy between high pretensions and low conduct.

Eventually the end of the wars of religion, as they are called, which followed on the heels of the Reformation, left Western Europe divided between Catholics and Protestants. Since the early seventeenth century there has been practically no alteration of the boundaries between the two confessions ; since the later seventeenth century no real expectation of any such. I will now endeavour, as I said above, to indicate some of the main differences between the respective ideals of Catholicism and Protestantism and their effects where they have been adopted.

No doubt the differences which are observable between peoples who are in the main Protestant and those who are in the main Catholic are to a large extent national or racial, but I am only here concerned to mention points which seem to be intimately connected with the difference between the two forms of Christianity.

Protestantism, as we have seen, aimed at the unification of the moral standard, and thus at making all life moral and religious alike. Thus, as has been remarked already, it abolished the technically "religious"—that is, the monastic—life, allowed the priest to be a married citizen, and was (in varying degrees) on the whole more or less indifferent or even hostile to the observance (with one marked exception, presently to be mentioned) of specially sacred times. In these results of Protestantism was involved the danger that where no part of life was to be specially religious it would be easy for none to be so ; and as regards morals, for the general standard, especially in regard of such virtues of secular social life as truthfulness, honesty, industry, economic independence, to be, on the whole, higher in Protestant countries than in Catholic, but what we may perhaps call *sanctity* to be rarer.

The retention of the technically "religious" or monastic life in Catholic countries, and of the modes of thought which go with it, have encouraged the more frequent appearance there of such special "sanctity"; but there is a greater danger, inherent in the very same circumstances, of inducing acquiescence in a lower standard for the mass of the people, especially in respect of such virtues as I enumerated above; for the extraordinary chastity of Catholic Ireland shows that in respect of that virtue, which has less direct connection with worldly activities, Catholicism need not fear comparison with Protestantism.

Again, the greater stress laid in Catholicism on religious observances seems to hinder the submergence of religious by secular interests, which is the special temptation of Protestantism. It is true that in some, though not in all, Protestant countries, a greater stress has been laid on one particular outward observance, that of the Lord's Day, than in Catholic countries. But this selection of one day in the week for strict observance, and abandonment (more or less) of other holy days, and even of religious worship on other days than Sunday, has tended in some respects to a more complete separation between the religious occupations of the Sunday and the undilutedly secular occupations of the rest of the week. In my own lifetime, however, I have seen a remarkable obsolescence of Sunday observance in this country, which makes this a matter of less present importance than it was even a very short while ago.

Again, Protestantism lends itself much more readily than Catholicism to the extension of religious diversity and non-conformity ; though this is more markedly true in the Anglo-Saxon than in the Teutonic and Latin lands which have adopted the Reformation. Why this should be it is easy to see. It is related of Queen Victoria that she once asked Lord John Russell whether he thought it was ever right for a subject to resist his Sovereign. "Speaking, madam," he replied, "to a Sovereign of the House of Hanover, I am bound to say 'Yes'!" In the same way as a Hanoverian monarch cannot consistently claim to receive a passive obedience from his subjects, a Protestant Church which has itself separated from the unity of Western Christendom, whose centre was at Rome, cannot so whole-heartedly discourage further separation as the Church which has never thus separated itself. Now, a result of this, the bearing of which on the politics of the present day is important, is that in Protestant countries—and especially, as I said, in Anglo-Saxon Protestant countries—there are many Churches, and the number tends (or has, until very lately, tended) to increase. Religion comes thus to be less closely associated in men's minds with one Church only, and opposition to one Church is not identified in men's minds with opposition to religion. In Catholic countries the reverse is the case. Hence the ordinary Frenchman identifies religion with the Roman Catholic Church, and the Roman Catholic Church with religion. To be religious is to be suspected of clericalism by one party ; to be anti-clerical is to be suspected of irreligion by the other.

Once more, Protestantism has been, on the whole, more favourable to freedom of thought than Catholicism. This is, I think, to be explained on the same principle as I illustrated before from the story of Lord John Russell's reply to Queen Victoria. It does not imply that Protestantism is in itself necessarily more philosophical than Catholicism. In some ways it may even be said to be less so. But in Protestant countries the resistance offered to freedom of thought by established dogma is necessarily less, because that dogma is itself the result of a comparatively recent criticism of a previously established dogma, than where it can at any rate be asserted that the established dogma has continued unchanged since the earliest times. We may add to this explanation that the spirit of freedom and of resistance to the established order, when once awakened in the ecclesiastical Reformation, naturally seeks outlets in other directions. Hence there is no doubt that intellectual progress has been actually much greater, on the whole, in Protestant countries than in Catholic ; but I do not think it equally true that Protestant theology has had in all respects the advantage in philosophical profundity, or Protestant religion the advantage in spirituality over its rival.

Now, it is to be observed that for the greater part of the time which has elapsed since the Reformation, England is to be reckoned, in the main, among Protestant countries ; and in respect of the comparisons I have instituted I do not think any qualification is necessary in applying them to England as a Protestant country ; but we must not overlook the presence in Anglicanism, the religious system to which the majority of Englishmen have adhered, of Catholic elements, which the Oxford Movement sought to reinforce, and which may often make generalizations about Protestantism inapplicable to the religion of this country.

§ 3. ANGLICAN ISOLATION

In the lectures to which I referred above on *A Century of Anglican Theology*[1] I called attention to a certain *isolation* as a note of Anglican theology, at least in the period from the close of the Civil War until quite recent days—an interval of some 250 years, during which it ran its course, on the whole, apart from any regular or continuous influence upon it either of contemporary Roman or of contemporary Protestant theology ; in no very close connection with the contemporary movements of European thought, and in a less

[1] Pp. 4 ff.

close than one might expect even with the main currents of English philosophical speculation. The Reformation had detached the Church of England from Rome ; the Civil War, by the severance which it caused between the Puritans, who had for a time overturned its polity, and the ultimate victorious upholders of its peculiar tradition—the most conspicuous features of which were its maintenance of the episcopal succession and its close association with the ancient monarchical constitution of the State—had detached it also from the Protestantism of the Continent. The Universities, where its ministers were trained, were closed to all but signatories of the Thirty-nine Articles. Thus isolated, it had few dealings with foreign Churches, although from time to time there was a movement of sympathy toward communities or individuals in whom was combined, as in Anglicanism, adhesion to the ancient episcopal organization of the Church with antagonism to the pretensions of the Roman Pontiffs. A scholar like the Prussian Lutheran Grabe, or like the French Calvinist Casaubon at an earlier date, might find in England an order more easily recognizable as continuous with that of the Church of the Fathers and Councils than the presbyterian constitution and unsacramental worship of their own original communions, though without the submission to claims which seemed to them no less remote from the primitive model. The Gallican Church, determined to resist papal en-

croachments, and relying in its resistance on the
support of a powerful Crown, was naturally not
wholly indifferent to the Anglican, which had
pushed the same line of conduct to the length of
making itself, under the royal supremacy, independent of the Roman Court. A certain sympa-
thetic interest in the ancient episcopal Churches
of the East which repudiated the supremacy of
the See of Peter was a recurring feature of
Anglican ecclesiastical life. The great religious
movement of the eighteenth century—that of
which the Wesleys and Whitfield were the pro-
tagonists—was undoubtedly indebted in its origin
to the influence of German Pietism and of
Moravianism ; but it assumed in England a
characteristically English form, both within and
without the Church in which it originated ; and
on the whole, as I have said, a certain isolation
characterized throughout the life and thought of
the Church of England. This isolation on the part
of Anglicanism has sometimes led to its being
practically overlooked by its neighbours. There
is a curious example of this in a modern work of
immense erudition, the *Soziallehren* of the late
Ernst Troeltsch. The knowledge shown in it of
English Nonconformity is remarkable ; but he
seems to regard the Anglican contribution to the
problems of religious social life and thought, so
far as he notices it at all, as little more than an
appendix to that of the bodies which in their
separation from her had linked themselves more

closely with the religious life of Continental Protestantism. A singular instance of this failure in a very eminent scholar and thinker to appreciate the place of the established Church of this country in the religious history of the nation is to be seen in the fact that, when speaking of the influence exerted by the great German mystic, Jacob Boehme, or Behmen, Troeltsch does not omit to mention a minute sect of Behmenist dissenters in England, but ignores the illustrious Anglican religious writer who in his later years devoted himself to the interpretation of Behmen's message, William Law, the author at an earlier period of one of our religious classics, *The Serious Call to a Devout and Holy Life,* as well as of some controversial works, whose intellectual force and literary merit have given them a permanent interest far beyond that to which the great majority of treatises on polemical theology can pretend.

§ 4. ANGLICAN PLATONISM

In my lectures, before quoted, on *A Century of Anglican Theology*[1] I mentioned Platonism as being one of the two salient characteristics of Anglican theology, its isolation, which I have now sufficiently described and discussed, being the other. The Oxford Movement certainly exemplifies its isolation ; less noticeably its Platonism.

[1] Pp. 7 ff.

The spirit of Oxford at that day had been moulded by Aristotle rather than by Plato : the intensive study of the *Republic,* which has been a feature of the school of *Literæ Humaniores* during living memory, was a later development, a development, however, which the Oxford Movement seems to have had its share in producing. The analogy between the ideal of a Christian Church with an hierarchy of divine institution controlling and inspiring all departments of life, which haunted the imaginations of the Anglo-Catholics (this name, now associated with what we may call the extreme right wing of the school which counts itself continuous with that of the Oxford Tractarians, was the one which these latter themselves, on the whole, preferred as their own designation), and that of the rule of the Philosopher-King adumbrated by Plato in the *Republic* attracted them to that great dialogue ; and the beginning of the regular lectures thereon, which have since become so important a feature of Oxford philosophical training, is said to have been due to an eccentric adherent of the Movement, William Sewell of Exeter, the founder of Radley College. But the Oxford Movement, on the whole, cannot be said especially to illustrate the Platonism which has been a recurrent characteristic of Anglican theology.

III

THE MORALISM OF THE OXFORD MOVEMENT

§ 1. English Moralism

IF, however, it is true, as on the whole it is, that Anglican theology was isolated from the general movement of European and even of English thought, so far as the latter took the form of definitely philosophical speculation, it, notwithstanding, as itself a phenomenon of English spiritual life, illustrated the characteristically English approach to the problems of life which Dr. Brilioth calls "moralism." Our foreign neighbours have been apt to accuse us English of *tartufferie,* or hypocrisy, as a national trait. I shall not pretend that the accusation is utterly without foundation ; but hypocrisy, even when real, is, as the proverb has it, a homage which vice pays to virtue ; and much that has passed for hypocrisy in English conduct is due rather to self-complacency and lack of imagination than to any conscious, still less deliberate, sophistication or dissimulation on our part. Englishmen have an instinctive sense of the importance of conduct, an instinctive admiration of moral excellence quite out of proportion to the value which they set upon beauty in art or upon profundity in thought ; and they are even apt to look with some suspicion on anything which they suspect to be an over-estimation of these latter. It is not an accident that Great Britain is distinguished by its remarkable output of work on moral philosophy during the seventeenth and eighteenth centuries ; and we shall find that emphasis on the importance of the moral consciousness as at once the root of religion and the test of its reality is the really essential feature of the Oxford Movement in its theoretical aspect. The Oxford Movement is a thoroughly English product ; and what makes Dr. Brilioth's admirable monograph especially remarkable is the sympathy with which he, though not an Englishman, has entered into the spirit of a Movement so emphatically English alike in its strength and in its weakness.

§ 2. CHRISTIANITY AND MORALITY

On the relation of Morality to Religion in general I have dwelt at length elsewhere, both in a book called *Problems in the Relations of God and Man*[1] and in a series of lectures on that express subject published in the same volume as those on *A Century of Anglican Theology*,[2] to which I have already several times referred. But I now turn to the consideration of the relation of

[1] Ed. 1915, pp. 101 ff. [2] Pp. 55 ff.

Morality, not to Religion in general but to the Christian Religion in particular. It is a subject with a very direct bearing upon the topic of Religious Thought in the Oxford Movement.

Unquestionably, Christianity is distinguished among the religions of the world by its emphasis upon morality. Holiness is for Christians the principal attribute of God; and "holiness" not understood in what was perhaps the primitive sense of this word and its equivalents, of a mysterious and uncomprehensible remoteness—the "otherness" upon which Professor Rudolf Otto has (onesidedly, as I venture to think) lately dwelt, as the *differentia* of the divine—but quite definitely as *ethical* perfection, the ideal of human conduct. "Be ye perfect, even as your Father which is in heaven is perfect."[1] The character of Jesus, as set before us in the Gospels, a character which unquestionably has beyond any other in history impressed men as supremely virtuous, is here regarded not merely as a manifestation of divinity, alongside of characters exhibiting excellencies of a quite different kind—as it might be, nay, certainly would be and indeed *is* regarded by adherents of the Hindu religion—but as the "glory" of the Only-begotten of the Father—the Word that is with God and is God—once for all made flesh, "full of grace and truth."[2] The Spirit of God is in Christian theology always the *Holy* Spirit—and just for this reason the identifi-

[1] Matt. v. 48.   [2] John i. 1 ff.

cation of this third Person of the Christian Trinity with the *Anima Mundi* of the kindred Platonic doctrine has never been accepted in Christian thought as satisfactory. On the other hand, Plato's canon, laid down by him in the *Republic*,[1] that no evil is to be attributed to God, so that tales in which this seems to be done must always be rejected—either as asserting of God what is not true of him, or as calling that evil what is indeed from him but is not truly evil—is whole-heartedly adopted by Christianity.

Hence arise certain problems which will be found to be important in the present connection. They arise from the difficulty found in reconciling the place assigned in Christianity to the moral consciousness as the organ of religious apprehension with (*a*) implications of the notion of revelation which seems to be essential to Christian doctrine ; (*b*) the personal relation with God to which Christianity invites its adherents. The difficulties raised under these two heads respectively are in a certain sense mutually opposed ; but they are connected as associated with that historical aspect with which the Christian religion cannot dispense altogether without becoming unrecognizable and losing its identity.

The notion of revelation inevitably suggests the possibility that what is *revealed* about God and authenticated by external evidences (*e.g.*, that of miracles) may *not* commend itself to the moral

[1] *Rep.* ii., 379 ff.

consciousness, which may then be called upon to submit itself to what it is not entitled to criticize ; while the analogy of our experience of mutual human relations induces the thought that personal devotion to the divine Author of the moral law may compensate in his sight for disobedience to his commandments.

To these suggestions, moreover, support may be lent both by the authority of the books reckoned sacred in the Christian community and by certain judgments of the moral consciousness itself which oppose themselves at least *prima facie* to others. The inclusion of the Old Testament in the canon of Scripture involved the presence there of statements about God belonging to an earlier level of spiritual development which the moral consciousness of a later generation had long left behind ; and in the New Testament there were stories which, at any rate, superficially taken, suggested that emotional attachment to him who was acknowledged as God manifest in the flesh might be set against conduct morally reprehensible. " Her sins, which are many, are forgiven her, for she loveth much."[1]

Moreover, humility and self-distrust themselves are felt to be moral virtues ; and a good man is not ready lightly to sit in judgment upon what he takes to be the actions of anyone wiser and better than he—and *a fortiori* not upon what he believes to be the actions of God ; while there

[1] Luke vii. 47.

is also felt to be something about personal love which exceeds in value, even in ethical value, mere obedience to a legitimate ordinance.

§ 3. KANT AND THE OXFORD MOVEMENT

Half a century before the Oxford Movement Kant had in his ethical works and in the treatise upon *Religion within the Limits of Mere Reason,* with which he followed them up, expounded a doctrine in which Religion became little more than an appendix to morality, and in which such factors in the Christian tradition should be gradually eliminated as seem to adulterate a purely ethical faith, either by the admixture of positive elements received merely on authority or by the assimilation of our attitude towards God as the imponent of the moral law revealed in conscience to that which we might have toward a human friend ; the former as relics of an outworn Judaism, the latter as the fruits of a fantastic enthusiasm which a fully mature reason would put away as unworthy. I am only here concerned with Kant's philosophy of religion so far as it seems to me that the Oxford Movement followed Kant, although no doubt unconsciously, in his emphasis on morality as the root of religion, while not following him in his indifference to history and the depreciation of the sentiment of personal devotion in religion which were unquestionably defects in his account of religious

D

experience; although we may doubt whether the Oxford divines succeeded in avoiding the pitfalls to escape from which Kant had thrown over history as a thing indifferent, and personal devotion as what he called *Schwärmerei*. With Kant's dread of the positive and arbitrary in religion as destructive of the ethical character, which for him alone entitled it to be considered as a *rational* state of mind, the Oxford divines would have had no sympathy. They did not only accept, they were specially interested in insisting upon the religious value of mystery and upon the authority of tradition in the religious life. In this they echoed the general reaction against eighteenth-century rationalism which inspired the Romantic movement of the first part of the nineteenth century; and it was just here that Kant was in sympathy with the earlier period which culminated in him, and which, by his drastic criticism of certain assumptions which it had made, he brought to an end. Nevertheless, the "moralism" of the Tractarians, to use Dr. Brilioth's expression, a tendency in which they showed themselves thoroughly English, and in which their attitude was in particular profoundly influenced by Butler, at that time, along with Aristotle, the great master of the Oxford philosophical school—and Butler's general ethical position was, of course, closely akin to that of Kant—eventually led their followers further in the direction of a criticism of tradition on ethical grounds than they themselves would have been willing to go. But of this here-after.

At present I would only call attention to the fact that they were quite opposed to Kant's attempt to eliminate from Christianity the positive and mysterious elements in the tradition of the Church. On the contrary, they were deeply concerned to insist upon the authority, not only of Scripture itself, but of its traditional interpretation, and upon the importance of sacraments as means of imparting divine grace to the soul.

These last—the authority of tradition and the importance of sacraments—were at the time called in question not only by rationalists, but by ultra-Protestants (to use a phrase commonly employed by Tractarian writers), who associated veneration for Church Fathers and for outward ceremonies with Popery; and this attitude was often combined with an emphasis on the Lutheran doctrine of justification by faith, which tended to disparage good works, any stress on which they suspected of implying reliance on one's own righteousness, and to exaggerate the importance of *feelings* which were taken as attesting the individual's assurance of his own salvation through faith in the Atonement offered by Christ on his behalf and in his stead. In their revulsion from this exaltation of pious feelings, with its encouragement of a peculiar phraseology that served to distinguish those who possessed these inward experiences from others, and also of a substitution of an emotional sense of personal intimacy with a divine Saviour for awe in the presence of the infinitely holy Giver of the Moral Law, the Tractarians would have found themselves at one with Kant, whose early upbringing in the German Pietism of his day (to which the English Evangelicalism of the early nineteenth century was nearly akin), while leaving enduring traces in his earnest and religious attitude towards life, inspired him with an intense dislike of the *Schwärmerei,* the morbid enthusiasm, as it seemed to him, of the sentimentalism in which it was apt to find compensation for the neglect of a whole-hearted endeavour to perform the everyday duties which we owe to ourselves and our neighbours.

Readers of the Tractarian literature must not be misled by the language sometimes used in it about the Evangelical disparagement of good works into supposing that English Evangelicalism was really, in practice, antinomian. As a matter of fact, it was unquestionably a power for righteousness ; and Newman, at any rate, who always dated his religious life from a conversion experienced in boyhood under Evangelical influence, never intended to deny this. But the theoretical disparagement by Evangelicals of good works and their preaching of justification by faith in language which could be construed to mean that they might be safely dispensed with both before and after justification, appeared to discourage that aspiration after personal holiness, and dissatisfaction with failure to attain it, which was the very soul of the piety cultivated by the Oxford teachers. In their aversion to any doctrine which would in any way weaken the conviction of the necessity of moral effort as the absolute pre-requisite and condition of any title to expect divine assistance, they were once more at one with Kant ; but in the value which they set upon sacraments as objective guarantees of grace actually conferred they parted company altogether with him.

§ 4. THE OXFORD MOVEMENT AND HOLINESS

It has been pointed out by more than one writer who has dealt with the Oxford Movement that the desire of *holiness* was its grand inspiration from first to last ; and this is the central truth about it. Accordingly, its leaders insisted in the first place —and here they were following Butler and agreeing with Kant—that the root of religion in general and of the Christian religion in particular was in the moral consciousness ; and that, therefore, except where a real effort to obey the moral law so far as known was present, no religious progress could be expected. In the second place, they urged that, although the moral consciousness, where not suppressed or perverted, would lead to conviction of sin and recognition of the need of

53

divine grace, yet the very purpose of that grace when given was to enable the recipient to progress further in sanctification, ever conscious, indeed, of his shortcomings, but ever striving after the pattern given in the Mount : "Be ye perfect, even as your Father which is in heaven is perfect."[1] They thought that the Evangelical party went astray, both as regards the root and as regards the flower of the Christian life. In their pre-occupation, with the Atonement as the essence of the Gospel, they tended, on the one hand, to despise the natural religion of obedience to the moral law, which the Gospel really presupposed, because it was not as yet conscious of its need of the Atonement ; and on the other hand, to stop short at the Atonement and ignore the issue of that taking of the manhood into God which made Atonement possible in the gradual hallowing of human lives through the actual presence of the divine life therein, whereby in the words of Newman's well-known poem (written, it is true, much later, in his Roman Catholic days, but true to the spirit of the theology of the Movement which he had led as an Anglican) :

> ". . . A higher gift than grace
> Should flesh and blood refine,
> God's presence and His very self
> And Essence all divine."[2]

No doubt, as one would expect, the Oxford divines did not all recognize with equal clearness

[1] Matt. v. 48. [2] Dream of Gerontius.

54

the essentials of their position, and no doubt the individual differences among them modify in various ways the form which it takes. But we may, I think, say in general that there is common to them all a refusal to treat the Atonement in isolation from the Incarnation, and a view of the Incarnation as involving an actual objective entry of the divine life into humanity, which is mediated in the case of individual men and women through the sacrament of Baptism, and issues in the gradual conformation of the individual Christian to the image of Christ.

§ 5. THE OXFORD MOVEMENT AND THE ATONEMENT

One of the most celebrated of the Tracts for the Times, on account of the censure it incurred from critics whose minds were full of the notion of a Popish plot, was the eightieth of the series, that on *Reserve in the Communication of Religious Knowledge,* from the pen of the gentle and saintly Isaac Williams, known for the genuine poetic vein exhibited in his *Baptistery* and *Cathedral* and in his contributions to the *Lyra Apostolica,* to which Keble, Newman, and Hurrell Froude were also contributors, and also for his devotional commentaries on the Gospels.

This tract was especially severe on the Evangelical fashion of preaching the doctrine of the Atonement. It was a principle with them, the author complained, that this, "the highest and most sacred of all Christian doctrines, is to be brought before and pressed home to all persons indiscriminately, and most especially to those who are leading unchristian lives." He denied that this practice had scriptural authority. St. Paul's "preaching of Christ crucified" he interpreted to mean "the necessity of our being crucified to the world." To "approach the Object" of our worship in prayer without holiness of life is, he said, "the object of every false or perverted religion"; and this he illustrated by the Roman Catholic "tendency to substitute the Virgin for God as the object of religious worship," which was an example of the way in which "the natural heart lowers the object of its worship to its own frailty." The indiscriminate preaching of the Atonement to all and sundry offended him as essentially irreverent; he had a feeling which may find expression in the words of a very different writer, from whom it would probably not have occurred to him to seek for support. In the second part of *Wilhelm Meister* Goethe introduces the Overseer of his Pedagogic Utopia, explaining why the last scene of our Lord's life is not included among the pictures from the New Testament which are painted in the gallery for the instruction of the pupils, but reserved in a "sanctuary of sorrow" for a later stage, when their education should have prepared them for it. "We draw a veil over those sufferings, even

56

because we reverence them so highly. We hold it a damnable audacity to bring forth that torturing Cross and the Holy One who suffers on it, or to expose them to the light of the sun, which hid its face when a reckless world forced such a sight on it, to take those mysterious secrets in which the divine depth of Sorrow lies hid, and play with them, fondle them, trick them out, and rest not till the most reverend of all solemnities appears vulgar and paltry."[1] But the Evangelical lack of this reserve, which even a poet so little of an orthodox Christian had felt suitable to the mystery of the Redeemer's death, had, in Williams's view, a directly mischievous effect on morality as suggesting that obedience was rather dispensed with by the offer of salvation through that death than presupposed by it in those to whom it should be made available. "There is no one living," he says—with a reference to Prov. viii., where the representation of Wisdom as crying "at the gates, at the entry of the city, at the coming in at the doors" might seem at first sight to suggest anything rather than the reserve in communicating religious truth which he was concerned to recommend—"There is no one living but to whom Wisdom speaks, a voice that tells him of something better which he ought to do than what he does. . . . Until he follows this first voice, the higher and better Wisdom is hid from him."

We come back, then, to what is unquestion-

---

[1] *Wilhelm Meister's Wanderjahr,* c. ii. (trans. Carlyle).

ably the fundamental thought of the Oxford teachers and the one in which they coincide with Kant, the thought of the moral consciousness as the true root of religion.

Different as were the emotional reactions which the doctrine of the Atonement produced in the very different minds of the philosopher of Königsberg and the gentle poet whom I have been quoting, there is a real affinity between the latter's desire[1] to withdraw the doctrine from the contemplation of all who have not first set their feet on the path of obedience and the former's insistence that, although God may, as the doctrine of the Atonement for human sin by his incarnate Son sets forth in a figure, see in our sincere but ever-imperfect obedience to the moral law that perfect holiness, the actual presence of the idea whereof in our practical reason is the motive and driving force of the moral effort which our subjection to the form of time hinders us from ever completing except by identification of ourselves in will with the eternal Sonship set before us in the New Testament picture of the life of the Founder of our religion, yet such continual moral effort is the sole condition of *our* being able to avail ourselves of this readiness of God to "accept us in the Beloved."[2] Moreover, with Kant also the

[1] See *Religion innerhalb der Grenzen der blosen Vernunft*, I., iii., § 7 (*Werke*, ed. Hartenstein, vi., 212 ff).

[2] Eph. i. 6.

Atonement is not isolated from the Incarnation ; the death of Christ is regarded only as the grand climax of the obedience of his life ; and it was an essential feature of the Oxford Movement that it made the Incarnation rather than the Atonement the central dogma of Christianity. This is a feature in which the later stages of the Anglo-Catholic movement have remained true to type ; as, for example, we see in the title[1] and contents of *Lux Mundi,* which represents its first attempt to come to terms with evolutionary thought and modern biblical criticism. It will at once be obvious that there is a real affinity between this subordination of the Atonement to the Incarnation in Tractarian as contrasted with Evangelical theology, and the emphasis of the former on obedience to the law given to conscience as the root of religion. For the death of Christ, when isolated from his life, tended to be regarded as a transaction revealing God's love to sinners in the substitution of his Son for them as the victim of his anger against their sins, rather than as the culmination of a life of perfect obedience which changed us from objects of God's wrath to objects of his love by the actual impartation to us, through the medium of the sacraments, of the divine-human life which it illustrated.

[1] " A Series of Studies in the Religion of the Incarnation."

§ 6. THE OXFORD MOVEMENT AND NON-CHRISTIAN RELIGION

This more concrete view, as we shall readily allow it to be, as it refused to isolate the Atonement from the general process of the Incarnation, so it refused to isolate the Incarnation itself from the general moral education of the human race. Accordingly, the deepest thinkers among the Tractarians took up the same general position against the "ultra-Protestants" of their day as Hooker had taken up against the Puritans of his, recognizing a certain sacredness in the traditions and customs of "natural religion" which forbade their absolute rejection on the ground that they were not specifically Christian, so long as they were capable of finding a place within the organic life of the Church without injury to its Christian character. There can be no question that in their respective attitudes to natural religion and piety we have here a real historical differentiation between what we may call the Catholic and Protestant tendencies in theology, and one in which the specifically Anglican tradition is, on the whole, Catholic rather than Protestant. The extravagances of the Ritschlian school in denying the kinship of Christian with natural theology— they culminate in Herrmann's doubts whether we can in the least enter into the religious experience of non-Christians[1]—are the exaggeration of a

[1] *Communion with God,* Eng. tr., pp. 61 ff.

Protestant tendency. It must be admitted, on the other side, that the greater readiness of Catholic theology to recognize the element which the Christian religious system, as being a religious system, has in common with others which are not Christian, places it in greater danger of subordinating those quite characteristically Christian values which distinguish the Gospel from every kind of "law," and upon which it has been the historical mission of Protestantism to insist.

In our study of the Tractarian literature we shall sometimes find language which does not seem quite consistent with what I have just been saying. There is some sharp criticism of contemporary writers, such as the well-known Scottish theologian, Erskine of Linlathen, who urged that the religious value of such a doctrine as that of the Trinity was to be found, not in the abstract doctrine as such in its difficulty and obscurity, but in its influence upon our feelings, and in its moral and practical implications. The writer's aversion to rationalism and to the attempts of those infected therewith to eliminate mystery from the creed of Christians was the ground of their suspicion of a line of thought which was later to be pursued by some of themselves. In the more speculative of these—in Hurrell Froude, for example ; in Newman (who was, however, himself the author of Tract 73, in which the strictures on Erskine occur which I have referred to) ; and in Ward—we find an explicit emphasis on the importance of connecting Christian doctrine with the deliverances of the universal moral consciousness and on the right of natural religion to be regarded as a divine dispensation, which, though it may have led them to conclusions not wholly acceptable to the less intellectually courageous of their school, is, I think, to be considered as the genuine development of an essential principle of Anglican, or at least of Anglo-Catholic, theology.

To illustrate what I have just said, I will quote a few passages from the three writers I have mentioned ; first, from Richard Hurrell Froude, who died of consumption in 1836, in his thirty-third year, perhaps, next to Newman, the most brilliant and original of the Oriel group which played so great a part in the Oxford Movement, and whose *Remains,* which Keble and Newman edited after his death, are among the most interesting parts of its literature. We find him[1] as early as 1827, when he was already a Fellow of Oriel, but had not yet taken Orders, expressing himself as follows : " I assent to the damnatory clauses of the Athanasian Creed because I believe them only to repeat the declaration of Scripture. I feel a difficulty in assenting because I admit, as a self-evident axiom, that no opinion can, *as such,* be the object of God's wrath or favour. The declaration and axiom are reconcilable on the supposition that the condemned opinion involves something

[1] *Remains,* i., 117.

moral as its effect or cause, or both." So in a sermon on "The Gospel as the Completion of Natural Religion,"[1] preached on Trinity Sunday, he declares that "the only possible way of understanding" the doctrines of the Trinity and the Incarnation "and profiting by them, or, indeed, of entering at all into their meaning, is by leading that sort of life which they are intended to help us in leading." It is certainly not easy to distinguish the position here implied from that of Erskine, denounced by Newman in Tract 73. He goes on, speaking of the affirmations of the Athanasian Creed : "We must ask ourselves, not 'Am I thoroughly convinced and certain that these mysterious doctrines are true?' for that is a matter over which we have no control ; we cannot feel certain by trying to feel ever so much ; and God will not require of us impossibilities. But what we must ask ourselves is this : 'Is my conduct such as it *would be* if I was thoroughly convinced of them ? In the first place, do I act as if I believed God to be my Father, and my neighbour to be my brother ?' That is, 'do I believe in earthly things ? (he is, of course, alluding to the words of Christ to Nicodemus in the Fourth Gospel[2]) and, secondly, as to heavenly things, do I *endeavour* with all my might and with all my soul, and with all my strength, to *follow and obey* the Lord Jesus Christ *as* my Saviour and my God?'" A student of Kant's philosophy of

[1] *Remains,* ii., 58 ff.   [2] John iii. 12.

religion cannot help being struck by the resemblance of such expressions to Kant's insistence on the essentially *practical* significance of religious doctrines.

Turning from Froude to Newman, we may observe a remarkable passage in a University Sermon preached in 1830 on "The Influence of Natural and Revealed Religion Respectively."[1] After a sketch of what he takes to be the religious knowledge attainable apart from revelation, he says : " Such is the large and practical religious creed attainable (as appears from the extant works of heathen writers) by a vigorous mind which rightly works upon itself under (what may be called) the Dispensation of Paganism. It may even be questioned whether there be any essential character of Scripture doctrine which is without its place in this moral revelation. For here is the belief in a principle exterior to the mind to which it is instinctively drawn, infinitely exalted, perfect, incomprehensible ; here is the surmise of a judgment to come ; the knowledge of unbounded benevolence, wisdom, and power, as traced in the visible creation, and of moral laws unlimited in their operation ; further, there is something of hope respecting the availableness of repentance, so far (that is) as suffices for religious thought ; lastly, there is an insight into the rule of duty increasing with the earnestness with which obedience to that rule is cultivated." It is

[1] *University Sermons,* p. 22.

appreciation of which is necessary to a right understanding of the Oxford Movement as a movement of religious thought. When Ward came to know Newman's teaching better and to compare it with Arnold's, "Arnoldism seemed," says his biographer,[1] "at every turn to stop short. . . . Intellectually it stopped short. . . . The principle of free critical inquiry . . . led . . . to scepticism . . . only Arnold would not carry it out consistently. . . . Again, practically Arnoldism stopped short. It loved to keep the supernatural at a distance. . . . And ethically it stopped short. . . . It had no saints. It watered down Christianity to what seemed more practicable for the average Christian than Christ's own teaching." I am not now concerned at all to examine the justice of the criticism here made upon what the writer calls "Arnoldism." Nor for the moment shall I pursue the thought for the sake of which I quoted it. This was the thought that the bulk of those—and there were, of course, many among the contemporaries of the Tractarians in the Church of England or outside of it—who sympathized with their insistence on the primacy of the ethical element in Christianity, presented, nevertheless, an unsatisfactory view of that religion, because they did not pass on from urging obedience to the voice of conscience in the conduct of ordinary life to the cultivation of a certain characteristic type of sanctity. This type

[1] *W. G. Ward and the Oxford Movement*, p. 86.

of sanctity appeared to the Tractarians to have been associated with Christianity in its most eminent representatives from its origin down to the Reformation, but after that event to have been, on grounds closely connected with inferences drawn from the Lutheran doctrine of justification, depreciated among Protestants, though still held in honour in the Roman Church. The recognition of the importance of this thought in the theology of the Oxford Movement is indeed essential to an understanding of its development, and so I took the opportunity afforded by my quotation from Wilfrid Ward's account of his father's passage from the school of Arnold to that of Newman to introduce it to my readers' notice. But I now return to passages illustrating, rather, Ward's agreement with Froude and Newman and the Oxford Movement generally in emphasizing the position of the moral consciousness as the soil wherein the roots of any religious experience must be struck which could hope to develop healthily after the Christian type.

Ward's chief work is the celebrated *Ideal of a Christian Church*, which was formally condemned by the University of Oxford in 1844 and the author deprived of his degrees. This book is full of assertions of the danger of any tampering (as he believed the Lutheran doctrine of justification to tamper) with "the truth," as he puts it,[1] "that careful moral discipline is the necessary

[1] *Ideal of a Christian Church*, p. vii.

foundation, whereon alone Christian faith can be reared." The principle to which he was irreconcilably opposed was "the principle . . . of making the intellect an arbiter of moral and religious truth instead of the conscience."[1] When he calls this "the Protestant principle," one is inclined to question his history ; and I remember how I heard Dr. Martineau in his old age claim that Catholics and Unitarians were united in opposition to the traditional Protestant distrust of reason in religion. But history was never Ward's strong point.

Some other declarations of Ward in the same sense as that which I have quoted may be added : "Two principles . . . seem to me," he says, "vitally important at the present time, the one, the absolute supremacy of conscience in moral and religious questions, the other the high sacredness of hereditary religion."[2] (Here we have an echo of a thought profoundly characteristic of the Romantic movement ; I shall return to it.) In a note, he condemns the English Reformation as much worse than the Continental in respect of its grasp of the former of these two principles. " No English Reformer," he declares, "exhibits the same 'single-minded and honest indignation' as Luther." The foreign Reformers *did,* he thinks, follow their consciences ; the English Reformers' notions were political. Here again the historian will hardly endorse his sweeping statement, and

[1] *Ideal,* p. 41 n.   [2] *Ibid.,* pp. 43, 44.

will probably reduce it to the concession that there was no individual English Reformer who ranks with Luther in what we may call individual prophetic genius.

Again : '' The sense of duty . . . is the one faculty which is visited by divine grace, and which under that grace leads us onward to salvation.''[1]

'' Men speak as though in some sense at least and in some degree, the Gospel were a *reversal* of the natural Law, instead of being solely and exclusively its *complement*.''[2]

'' If conscience be not on all moral and religious subjects paramount, then it does not really exist ; if it do not exist, we have no reason whatever, nay, no power whatever, to believe in God. . . . The very argument on which M. Comte grounds his Atheism is . . . the circumstance that (as he considers) we have no such faculty as a conscience.''[3]

'' To do what is right because it *is* right, and from a motive of duty is the highest and noblest of all habits . . . far nobler than the doing what is right out of gratitude for free pardon.''[4] This is a truth, he says, '' which the abstract Lutheran doctrine denies and the practical Lutheran doctrine disparages.'' This last passage is very Kantian in tone. I conclude with one more extract from the *Ideal* which is specially striking when one remembers that the writer is in

[1] *Ideal,* p. 204.   [2] *Ibid.,* p. 248.
[3] *Ibid.,* p. 277.   [4] *Ibid.,* p. 301.

this book mainly concerned to exalt the ideal of a Church such as he was coming—or had come—to think the Roman Church alone was in actual fact.

"The priest of a country parish . . . will endeavour to lay his foundation within the heart of his flock ; he will not consider any attendance of theirs on Divine Service, even the most regular, even (if so be) daily as well as on Sunday, to be any real security for so much as the beginning of a truly Christian life. It is the feeling of *accountableness* throughout the day, the habitual thought of judgment to come, the careful regulation of thoughts, words, and actions, which he will impress on his flock as the one thing needful. Their presence in church may be useful as giving him the power to address them, but he will use that power for the very purpose of impressing on their mind that the true religion must have its spring from *within*."[1]

§ 7. INWARDNESS CHARACTERISTIC OF THE OXFORD MOVEMENT

Anglo-Catholicism has so often been regarded by those out of sympathy with it as essentially a religion of outward ordinances that perhaps it is with a certain surprise that some will note this last emphatic phrase. And yet, as a matter of fact, anyone who will be at the pains to familiarize himself with the literature of the Oxford Move-

[1] *Ideal*, p. 438.

ment will be disposed to think that *inwardness* was one of its principal notes. Its greatest leader, Newman, was, of course, pre-eminently a man of the inner life. He was one of the world's great autobiographers whose master interest was a drama whose actors were those "two only supreme and luminously self-evident beings, himself and his Creator," in the thought of whom, as he tells us in a famous passage of his *Apologia*.[1] he had come to rest since his conversion at the age of fifteen. The second title of this, his chief work, was "A History of my Religious Opinions," but a great part of his writings might, in fact, be equally so described ; and these religious opinions of his were always envisaged in these writings (and that is what gives them their peculiar fascination), not so much in the character of objective convictions, reached by research or argument, as in that of inward experiences, stimulated it might be now by the discovery of some fact of history, now by some train of reasoning, but revealed to the discoverer or reasoner himself as changes which had passed over his mood and given a different colour to the world around him. This was, of course, due to the idiosyncrasy of the individual John Henry Newman ; but the literature of the movement from the *Christian Year* onward is above all things the expression of an interior piety, whose very reliance on the assurance given by outward sacramental

[1] *Apologia*, p. 59.

signs of the real presence of inward spiritual grace is associated with a characteristic distrust of the value of feelings which will bear exposure to the public view. It shows a very just appreciation of this intimate retiring nature of Tractarian piety when Principal Shairp of St. Andrews, in his admirable essay on Keble,[1] fixed on these lines of his as expressing its inmost heart :

> " God only and good Angels look
> Behind the blissful screen ;
> As when triumphant o'er his foes
> The Son of God at midnight rose
> By aught but heaven unseen."

It is often, perhaps usually, the case that when we contrast two types of equally genuine spiritual experience we find a law of compensation, as we may call it, at work, in virtue of which any factor missing in one from the place it occupies in the other will be found in the first though in a different place, a place whence it is missing in the other. So in the present instance, while Evangelicalism seemed to disparage external means of grace as interposed between God and the soul in favour of a direct emotional acceptance by the individual soul of Christ as the Saviour whose righteousness is imputed to us who have none of our own, Tractarianism disparages individual feelings in favour of sacraments as efficacious vehicles of grace, but insists that through these material channels the righteousness of Christ is not merely

[1] Published in his *Studies in Poetry and Philosophy*.

73

imputed but imparted to us—that our *justification* is a making us, not a mere counting us, righteous, and is distinguished from *sanctification,* not as a wholly distinct process but as the beginning of a process from the continuance or completion of the same.

This is precisely what Wesley said.

IV

TRACTARIAN DOCTRINE OF JUSTIFICATION

§ 1. NEWMAN ON JUSTIFICATION

THE doctrine of Justification associated with the Oxford Movement is worked out in Newman's lectures on the subject, to which Dr. Brilioth rightly directs his readers' attention as the chief contribution of the Tractarian school to systematic theology. The student of the subject must read these discourses for himself—it is impossible here to give an adequate account of them. But the teaching contained in them is memorably summarized by the author himself in the following words : "Whether we say we are justified by faith or by works or by Sacraments, all these but mean this one doctrine, that we are justified by grace, given through Sacraments, impetrated by faith, manifested in works,"[1] and in a very learned Appendix he explains the relation of his view to others which had obtained currency in various theological schools : (1) " It has been said that we are justified directly upon our holiness and works wrought in us *through* Christ's merits by

[1] P. 348.

the Spirit ; or (2) upon our holiness and works *under* the covenant of Christ's merits ; or (3) that our faith is mercifully appointed as the substitute for perfect holiness, and thus is the interposing and acceptable principle between us and God ; or (4) that Christ's merits and righteousness are imputed as ours, and become the immediate cause of our justification, superseding everything else in the eye of our Judge. Of these the first is the high Roman view, the last the high Protestant, and the two intermediate are different forms of what is commonly considered the High Church view among ourselves, and very nearly resemble Bucer's among the Protestants and that of Pighius, Mussus, and many others among Romanists.''[1]

At first sight the second and third of these views might not seem to be so nearly the same as Newman appears to wish us to regard them as being. But his objection to what he here calls the ''high Roman'' view was that he understood it, although affirming that the Atonement wrought on our behalf by Christ was the sole ground of our good works, yet to deny the need of a continual imputation of Christ's merits to supply the defects of our actual obedience ; and hence he is indifferent whether we think of ourselves as justified by our holiness and good works, but of these as only effective because all through we lay hold by faith upon the grace of Christ, whose merits

[1] P. 394.

continually supply in God's sight the defects of our own obedience ; or of ourselves as justified by this very faith operating in the way described to make good, so far as it lies in our power to do, those same defects of our obedience. What he desires to oppose is, on the one hand, any reliance on the merit of our own good works as such ; on the other, any such mere reliance as he found in what he calls the "high Protestant" view on the imputation of the merits of Christ in substitution for our obedience, that subsequent effort on our part, after the greatest holiness attainable by us, becomes unnecessary, and even suspect, as suggesting some doubt of the sufficiency of Christ's atonement.

§ 2. IMPUTATION AND IMPARTATION

Now, here we come again in view of a feature of Tractarian piety which I have already mentioned, but did not then dwell upon—viz., its aspiration after such an unearthly holiness as the Christian's union with his divine Master, his incorporation in the mystical body indwelt by the divine Spirit, seemed to promise as possible to the heirs of such transcendent privileges. This characteristic aspiration is, of course, congruous with, but yet to be distinguished from, its insistence on the necessity of *obedience* as a preliminary to justification. Now, Luther's doctrine of justification was rooted in Luther's own religious experience of his failure to find spiritual peace in a life of aspiration after just such an unearthly holiness presented as the ideal of the monastic vocation which had been his own. Modern historical criticism has, indeed, thrown doubt upon the accuracy of Luther's later memories of his earlier religious life ; but this does not affect the fact that his doctrine of Justification reflected an experience which he at least believed to have been his own.

According to what he, at any rate, came to consider was the monastic ideal—an ideal which he held to be, in principle, the same with that of the Stoics—a Christian was at every moment striving to render himself a specimen, so to say, as perfect as possible in every detail, of the character of holiness which is acceptable in the sight of God. His own continual failure to succeed in this uphill work deprived him of the peace of conscience, which he eventually found, by the help of his study of St. Paul, in the doctrine of justification by faith in Christ, whose perfect obedience is *imputed* to those who thus believe in him. Such imputation is "forensic," as it is called ; it is an *accounting* righteous, apart from any question whether or how far the person thus accounted righteous *is* actually righteous or no.

No good works of ours, whether done before justification or after, can contribute to the forgiveness of sins, which is offered freely by Christ

to all who believe ; a forgiveness which is one
with what is called justification, for by the same
act God takes away our sins and accounts us
righteous for Christ's sake. *Accounts* us
righteous, not (we must note) necessarily *makes*
us righteous. In interpreting St. Paul's δικαιοῦν
as meaning to *account* or *declare* righteous not,
as the Latin *justificare* by its formation suggested
to the Latin schoolmen, to *make* righteous,
Luther would be supported by the majority of
scholars. The thought that God, for Christ's
sake, forgave us, not (at least in the initial stage)
by imparting or infusing his righteousness into us,
but by imputing it to us, so that it is in no sense
ours but only *his,* was the thought which alone
corresponded to the type of religious experience
which was exemplified by Luther, and of which he
recognized the record in St. Paul's Epistle to the
Romans. It finds familiar and noble expression in
Toplady's great hymn :

> " *Nothing* in my hand I bring ;
> Simply to thy Cross I cling :"

In contrast to this insistence on *imputation,*
Newman and the Tractarians, as Dr. Brilioth
notes in his valuable chapter,[1] laid a greater stress
on *gratia infusa*. Although Newman had himself
experienced a conversion, of the reality of which
he was still, when he wrote the *Apologia,* "more

---

[1] Ch. xiv. of his *Anglican Revival,* on the Doctrine
of Justification.

certain than that he had hands and feet,"[1] an
experience undergone at so youthful an age—he
was only fifteen—necessarily differed from those
which underlay the Lutheran theology in that it
had not been preceded, as with St. Paul and
Luther, by the prolonged efforts of a mature
person to reach peace of mind by means of an
endeavour to perform all the demands of an exact-
ing law. Newman's own conversion, moreover,
which, of course, occurred while he was under
the influence of a quite different school of piety
from that the traditions of which the Tractarians
were concerned to revive, was by no means typical
of his school. He is the only one of the three
great leaders of whom such an experience is
recorded. Pusey, indeed (says Dr. Brilioth[2]),
"brought with him from the Evangelical sphere
an intense and tender theology of the cross";
and we find him in a remarkable sermon on Conversion,[3] while affirming that a man may have
never lost the grace of baptism, or that if he has
he may turn again to God without being able to
name the date, yet adding emphatically : "In
whatever way a change may be wrought, a
change there must be"—(in all, that is, who
have fallen from baptismal grace, and these constitute, of course, the vast majority). "We may
not have turned to God," he goes on, "in the
same way, but whoever has turned from God and

---

[1] P. 59. [2] P. 242.
[3] *Parochial and Cathedral Sermons*, pp. 16 ff.

is now turned to Him must know if he once neglected God and now he seeks Him. . . . This is a marked change which the soul cannot but know." I do not know exactly in what sense Dr. Brilioth speaks of Pusey bringing his theology of the cross "from the Evangelical sphere"; he was not an Evangelical by family tradition, although his travels in Germany and intercourse in student days with German divines familiarized him with the literature of German Pietism. But, from whatever source he himself derived it, there can be no doubt that from Pusey, rather than any other of the Oxford leaders, came a certain strain which may conveniently be called "Evangelical" in the religion of the party which they led, and which has been more prominent in the later than in the earlier generations of the Movement. Those affected thereby have not shared the shrinking from the word "conversion," which some of us can remember in households with Tractarian traditions, where its use, except of the passage from infidelity to Christianity and from a life of open sin to one of moral respectability, was felt to involve some disparagement of the reality of baptismal grace. In such circles there was but scant sympathy for such a "High Church Methodist" (I remember the nickname being applied to him) as George Wilkinson, Vicar of St. Peter's, Eaton Square, and afterwards Bishop, first of Truro and then of St. Andrews. Thus it was not altogether without surprise that I myself, coming from such surroundings to Oxford forty years ago, found a quite different attitude in such a younger representative of the Tractarian tradition as the distinguished person who was then newly established as first Principal of Pusey House, and is now Bishop Gore. For here was none of that instinctive distrust of Evangelical language about individual conversion occurring in the case of persons already professing and practising Christians which characterized the school of thought in which I had been brought up. This attitude of Mr. Gore's, however, was, as I now recognize, less novel among Anglican High Churchmen than it then seemed to me ; it could appeal, as Dr. Brilioth well brings out, to the authority of Pusey himself. But it was, I still think, not typical of that High Church Movement, as it had by then established itself far and wide in the parsonages of the country, creating an atmosphere of piety, profoundly serious and dutiful, and at the same time cultured and reticent, restrained in the expression of emotion, but uncompromising in its acceptance of the Church's system as of divine authority ; an atmosphere which reminds us rather of the personality of the senior of the three Tractarian leaders, the author of the *Christian Year*, than of that of either Newman or Pusey.

It was a feature of the whole Movement, and one which was closely bound up with the dissatisfaction of its scholars with the Lutheran doctrine of Justification, that the Incarnation rather than the Atonement was the centre of its theology. As I have throughout attempted to show the analogies of the tendencies of thought implied in the Oxford Movement to contemporary tendencies in wider spheres, I will here take occasion to point out an analogy in the difference between Tractarian and Evangelical theology in this respect with the difference between the Hegelian and the Kantian positions. At first sight the Kantian philosophy of morality and religion seems un-Evangelical and un-Lutheran in its stress on the all-importance of a man's moral conduct and its aversion to any doctrine of relying on divine aid in substitution therefor ; nor is this difference between the two doctrines by any means unimportant. But between Luther's emphasis on *fides informis* in contrast with *fides formata caritate* as the sole justifying principle, and Kant's doctrine of *the goodwill,* which wills no particular act, but merely its own universality, as the sole principle of morality in human actions, there is a striking and significant correspondence. And the Hegelian recognition of the world of social institutions as the progressive self-realization of the principle presented by Kant as merely an obligation which may for ever remain unfulfilled, is echoed, as regards religion, by the Tractarian insistence on the system of Church and Sacraments as the body and expression of the divine life, the extension and elaboration, as it were, of its primary and personal incarnation in the humanity of Jesus Christ. Again, Kant stops short at the hope, suggested by the very urgency of the "ought" of the moral law which implies the "can" on the part of its subject, that the ideal of a perfect humanity apprehended by us as our ideal and taken as the model of our conduct will be in God's sight reckoned as fulfilled by that unceasing approximation to perfection beyond which the nature of time forbids us, as members of the phenomenal world, to aspire. Similarly, Evangelicalism tended to stop short with the acceptance of Christ as our Saviour, who has died *for* us. On the other hand, Hegel bids us see in society, as it has actually come to be, the real embodiment of the ideal, which apart from it is but an ineffectual dream. Similarly, the Tractarians offer us the divine-human life of Christ, imparted to us through the Church and its sacraments, and expressing itself in us, apart from which impartation and indwelling the mere acceptance of him by faith as our substitute leaves *us* still unrighteous. No doubt it is only through such substitution of his righteousness for ours that the forgiveness of our sins which enables us to start afresh is possible, and only through the faith which apprehends him as our Saviour can we open a free course to the grace which we received, before we could individually make an act of faith, in the sacrament of Baptism. But there is, notwithstanding, here a real analogy between Kant and the Evangelicals on the one hand, between Hegel and the Tractarians on the other.

To Kant the rites of common worship were no means of grace, but, at the best, means of mutually encouraging moral and religious sentiments in those who took part in them ; and any doctrine of sacraments which would raise them above the rank of suggestive ceremonies and allow to them any objective efficacy in the spiritual life was, in his view, inconsistent with that maintenance of individual independence and freedom from any law but that of conscience, which was to him the essential presupposition of genuine morality. We owe him unquestionably a great debt for his uncompromising insistence on this heritage of freedom ; but we observe that he was a true son of the individualistic and rationalistic Enlightenment, the reign of which he himself, by his destructive criticism of its assumptions, brought to a close, and showed that he was so in the slight attention which he paid to that unconscious or subconscious factor in our personality upon which much recent psychology has laid an at least equally one-sided stress, sometimes sacrificing, indeed, in its interest that very claim to rational freedom which Kant so impressively defended. That the individual life is rooted in the social, and is only by degrees appropriated by the individual, he did not fully recognize, and tended to treat association as something, in the first instance, perilous to individual morality, so that the origin of the Church or Kingdom of God is traced by him to the need of counteracting this peril of *evil* communications by the deliberate formation of a society aiming at mutual encouragement in *goodness*. Now, the action of sacraments is essentially *social;* it is distinguished in this way from *magic,* which is conceived of as affecting individuals physically as things and not as persons. An inadequate attention to those factors in personality which are at any time "below the threshold of consciousness" (as the modern phrase goes) will always go with an inadequate recognition of the place of sacraments in the spiritual life and a tendency to confuse them with merely magical operations, a tendency which, of course, appears, not only among disparagers, but among partisans of sacramental religion, and which in both cases depends upon an exaggerated individualism, an insufficient realization of the social nature of personality.

The identification of what are really mutually complementary factors in moral and religious experience, with schools, parties, or Churches devoted to their respective exposition, has often obscured, in the course of the history of ideas, the fact that religion lives in and by the tension between them, the disappearance of which through the suppression of one or the other must bring with it the impoverishment and ultimate mortification of that life itself. We are now becoming more ready to admit this truth, and the consequence of this is a wider prevalence of mutual study and understanding between the exponents of various points of view, which gives promise of a more genuine reunion than was possible while loyalty to one point of view was so often thought to demand hostility to that which is its complement.

Thus in the present case we have to recognize that it will not do to dwell, as Luther sometimes seems to do, on the "justifying" *fides informis* as though, without its expression of itself in love, it could be the faith that justifies at all ; or, as Kant sometimes seems to do, on the *goodwill* that alone is without qualification good, as though, if it willed nothing in particular, it could be truly good at all.

But we have also to recognize that the power of faith to give a new start to the penitent convinced of sin is independent of any estimation of merit in the works wherein that faith finds expression ; and that, however the institutions of society mediate to the individual the acquisition of the good disposition, it is the disposition alone that has moral value, not conformity to the habits created by the institutions, without the disposition or in addition to the disposition, as though the disposition were imperfect apart from such conformity as an empirical fact.

We must acknowledge the emergence of personality from social solidarity, and its essentially social nature from first to last ; but we must not in so doing forget—what is in no sense contradictory of these truths—that the very meaning of its emergence and of its place in the life of society lies in that freedom of which Luther and Kant, though using different kinds of language, alike stood forth as the apostles, and which is the inalienable privilege of personality.

"Luther," says Newman, "found Christians in bondage to their works and observances; he released them by his doctrine of faith; and he left them in bondage to their feelings."[1] Reformers are apt rather to see in the teachers to whom those appeal whose ways they hold themselves sent to reform the source of the evils which they are combating than to form an unbiassed judgment of them as they were. As Bacon saw in Aristotle chiefly the idol of a degenerate scholasticism, so Newman sees in Luther the patriarch of the tendency which, in much of the Methodist and Evangelical preaching of his day, seemed to him to identify justifying faith with an emotional crisis, compared with which both obedience to the moral law and aspiration after the holiness of life to which the Christian is called fell, as it were, into the background. The Tractarians revolted from the confident "assurance" of personal salvation in which Evangelicals seemed sometimes content to rest, and in contrast with this they encouraged and cultivated a constant sense of their own unworthiness, under which they might "work out their own salvation with fear and

[1] *Lectures on Justification,* p. 389.

trembling." On the other hand, if here they might be accused by their opponents of not claiming the peace of mind which might have been theirs, had they been willing to think less of their own works and accept the salvation freely offered by Christ to faith without works, they did not by any means acknowledge that their critics rather than they had learned the secret of Christian joy. Was not the belief in a mere *imputation* of Christ's merits a "joyless shadow" in comparison with the joy that came from the consciousness that there was actually *imparted* to them, infused into their souls, through the sacraments, the new life of the risen Christ himself?

Of the *risen* Christ; for it is true, as Dr. Brilioth has observed, that it is a feature of Tractarian piety that in it (I quote Dr. Brilioth[1]) "the thought of sharing in the glory of the risen Lord preponderates over confidence in the atoning work of the Cross," that "Easter overshadows Good Friday and makes its message only a part of its own"; and, moreover, that this "undoubtedly is a revival, not merely a mechanical reproduction, of the primitive feeling." He cites, along with other passages from Keble and Pusey, the words of Newman in his *Lectures on Justification*:[2] "If the Resurrection be the means by which the Atonement is applied to each of us, if it be our justification" (he is, of course, thinking of what we read in the Epistle to the Romans,[3]

[1] P. 289.   [2] P. 254 f.   [3] iv. 25.

that Christ " was delivered for our offences and was raised again for our justification "), " if in it are conveyed all the gifts of grace and glory which Christ has purchased for us, if it be the commencement of His giving Himself to us for a spiritual sustenance of His feeding us with that Bread which has already been perfected on the Cross and is now a medicine of immortality " (the famous phrase, φάρμακον ἀθανασίας is taken from one of the earliest of Christian writers, Ignatius, in his Epistle to the Ephesians[1]), " it is that very doctrine "—*i.e.,* the doctrine of the Resurrection —" which is most immediate to us, in which Christ most closely approaches us, from which we gain life, and out of which issue our hopes and duties."

This theory of Justification, then, favoured by Newman and the Tractarians, understands by the word less the *imputation* to us of the righteousness exhibited by Christ in his death than the *impartation* to the soul and *infusion* into it of the righteousness of Christ, processes which depend directly on the exaltation at the Resurrection of his humanity from the state of mortal weakness which, during his life on earth, he shared with all other individual men, to the state of immortal power, in which it is able to become the principle of spiritual life within those who are mystically united to him. The opponents of the Oxford Movement have often tended to see in it chiefly

[1] C. xx.

a reaction to medievalism, and that certain aspects and stages of it may be so described is not to be denied. But more characteristic is its return to a primitive consciousness of organic participation in the risen life of Christ, with which the concentration of Western medieval piety on the Passion has less in common than it has with Evangelical devotion to the Precious Blood. Even in the emphasis laid by the Tractarians on the Eucharist, in which it is at one with medieval theology, the Sacrament is envisaged by them, perhaps, on the whole, more predominantly as the food of the new life than as so often in the imagination of the medieval Latin Church as the mysterious reiteration of the sacrificial death, wherein at any moment a celebrant might (as in such miracles as that of Bolsena, immortalized by Raphael) have his faith confirmed by finding in his hands, instead of the species of bread which was but a mere appearance, a bleeding human body. We must, of course, be on our guard against overlooking in any of the variations of sentiment and teaching respecting the Christian mysteries the presence of elements with which we are more familiar in other contexts, and so doing injustice to the actual fulness of religious experience, whether in the primitive Church or in the Latin Church of the Middle Ages, among the spiritual children of the Reformation or in the Anglo-Catholic school which we are now studying. But it is none the less instructive to note what is most characteristic of each form of devotion ; and though, no doubt, among Anglo-Catholics some have been more, some less, attracted by the religion of the Western Church in the Middle Ages, I think it is true to say that the theological orientation of the Oxford Movement was, in accordance with the older tradition of the Anglican High Church party, rather toward that of the Fathers of the primitive Eastern Church, and that the attitude of its individual representatives toward the existing Roman Church was largely determined according as they were more impressed—as Newman came to be—with its faithfulness, in contrast to the Churches of the Reformation, although amid much unlikeness, to the type of the early Church, or, on the other hand, with its departure from the same type in contrast with the Church of England, as it presented itself in the writings and traditions of its High Churchmen, from Hooker, Andrewes, and Laud onwards to the time of the Tractarian movement itself.

§ 3. BAPTISMAL REGENERATION

It is easy to see why, if this is true, the doctrine of Baptismal Regeneration became of such central importance for the theology of the Tractarians. No doubt from the first a greatly increased reverence for, and use of, the other sacrament was an important feature of their religious life, but it was round Baptism rather than round the Eucharist that controversy raged at first. The significance of Baptism and its relation to justification are ever to the fore in the discussions between the Tractarian divines and their critics ; the constant emphasis, for example, in Keble's poetry on baptismal purity and the insistence on the peculiar gravity of post-baptismal sin are at once characteristic of the Movement and reminiscent of the preoccupations of the theologians of the primitive Church. It will be desirable for us to attend for a while to the meaning and importance of the doctrine of Baptismal Regeneration as affirmed by the Tractarians, and its relation to their view of justification.

V

BAPTISMAL REGENERATION

§ 1. DOCTRINE OF BAPTISMAL REGENERATION

It has to be borne in mind that baptism for St. Paul and the New Testament writers meant the solemn voluntary act of the mature person, who thereby definitely enrolled himself as a member of the Christian community. The association of it with the forgiveness of sins, which the washing of the new convert with water vividly symbolized, as he descended, as it were, with Christ into the river of death and rose again from its cleansing stream to share his new life among his followers, was natural and inevitable. Where, in point of fact, there were never disjoined from one another the faith of the convert, his public profession of it, the ceremony of his admission to the Church, the birthday of his new life as a Christian, whose sins were pardoned and himself declared righteous through his investment with Christ's righteousness, there was no need for curious inquiry as to the precise relation to each other of the various factors and aspects, external and internal, of the one grand action in which a man turned from darkness to light, from sin to righteousness, from the Kingdom of Satan to the Kingdom of God. It is otherwise when we are dealing with the child of Christians, born into a Christian community, and baptized as an infant, without any choice in the matter or any consciousness of the nature and meaning of the rite to which he was submitted. What, in such a case, was the relation of his baptism to such conversion as he might undergo at a later period? If he should ever begin to live a new life of conscious union with God instead of one of religious indifference or even of definite violation of moral laws, was not this, rather than the unconscious reception of a symbolic sprinkling which had meant nothing to him then or afterwards, his "regeneration"? And could one baptized in infancy, who should never display in his life any sense of religion at all, be said with any propriety to be "regenerate" at all? Yet the authorized formularies of the Church unquestionably affirmed that the baptized, as such, were regenerate; and the institution of infant baptism, so far from being due to any intention of converting into a mere outward rite of initiation into the community what had been originally the outward and visible sign of a new relation of the individual soul to God, was rather motived by the desire of Christians to secure to their children as early as possible this same new relation, on which the most momentous consequences, in this life and the next, were held to hang. These questions were further complicated with that of the relation of baptism to that predestination to life by the eternal will of God, which the teaching of St. Paul seemed to represent as the necessary condition of ultimate salvation, and which no one was prepared to assert could be presumed in all the baptized.

§ 2. Tractarian Emphasis on Baptismal Regeneration

The Tractarians, as has been already remarked, were confronted with a phase of Evangelicalism which appeared to them to make *feeling,* which is individual, subjective, variable, and only imperfectly under the control of the will, the test of justification; and in opposition to this the ancient language which connected justification with baptism commended itself to them as securing to the Christian the opportunity of participation in the divine-human life of Christ, independently of and prior to any such excitation of feeling as those they were criticizing seemed to regard as essential to the obtaining of the status of children of God and inheritors of his promises.

A hasty critic of this position might at first see in this merely a substitution, from the ethical point of view, thoroughly reactionary, of ceremonial purity, conferred by a rite in which the recipient, who in the vast majority of cases was baptized in infancy, was not even a conscious subject of the operation, still less a voluntary agent, for a genuine spiritual act of the individual convinced of sin and embracing for himself by faith the offer of salvation. But in the thought of the Tractarians the *ethical* advantage was all on the side of their position. The Evangelical appeal encouraged sinners simply to put aside obedience to the moral law as something with which the vicarious sacrifice of Christ accepted by faith had dispensed ; while, on the other hand, a genuine conviction that in baptism he had been actually "born again," that there had been imparted to him the new life of the risen Christ with all its power to achieve holiness, was calculated at once greatly to encourage an obedience towards which this grace infused into him by baptism could supply so powerful an aid, and immensely to heighten the gravity of sins committed by those who had been, in the words of the writer to the Hebrews, "enlightened" and had "tasted of the heavenly gift."[1] No Tractarian utterance startled and dismayed more than a famous sermon of Pusey on the "irreparableness of post-baptismal sin." Moral laxity was the last thing in the world associated in the mind of the Tractarians with their insistence on the prerogatives of the sacrament of baptism. In this matter they were, in fact, not very far from the position of Luther himself in his treatise on the *Babylonish Captivity,* where he assails the Church of his day for dis-

[1] Heb. vi. 4.

paraging baptism by its exaltation of subsequent vows, insists upon the assurance of salvation to all who believe and are baptized, and holds that the faith of the Church replaced, in the case of baptism, that of the individual, even as the paralytic man in the Gospel was healed by the faith of others.

But while we must entirely acquit the Tractarians of any concession to an unethical view of the Christian status in their emphasis on infant baptism as a true regeneration, and as the actual instrument of justification—for it was in quite the opposite character that it appealed to them, as bound up with that insistence on the indispensableness of obedience to the moral law which, rightly or wrongly, they missed in current Evangelicalism—this must not, of course, prevent us from recognizing how easily such a doctrine as theirs can be perverted into one which confounds sacramental with magical efficacy by allowing the former, abstracted from its relation to a sacred society, to exist where voluntary and personal activity on the part of the beneficiary is absent.

It would generally be allowed that the strength of the objection made to infant baptism by those who are called Baptists lies in the obvious unreality of employing the high language of Scripture about those who, in *their* baptism, had definitely broken with the world, the flesh, and the devil and enlisted themselves under the banner of Christ to describe persons who have been as a matter of social routine submitted in unconscious infancy to a traditional ceremony and have grown up quite without any sense of having committed themselves to any manner of life other than that suggested by the ordinary conventions of the society around them. Thoughtful apologists of infant baptism would admit that, apart from a genuine guarantee of Christian upbringing, infant baptism is a mockery, all the more profane the less it is thought of as a mere ceremony and the more there is attributed to it, at least potentially, a supernatural efficacy. The real defence against a superstitious view of sacraments is not a reduction of them to the position of mere outward ceremonies, having no organic connection, if one may so express oneself, with the spiritual experiences which they symbolize, but a grasp of their social character and of sociality as an essential feature of spiritual life.

The Tractarians would, no doubt, have denied, and justly denied, that they overlooked the social character of sacraments ; the sacraments were the sacraments of the Church, and it was not only Ward whose imagination was filled with an '' Ideal of the Christian Church '' as that which it was the mission of his school to realize in his native country.

> '' I will not cease from mental strife,
>   Nor shall my sword sleep in my hand
>   Till I have built Jerusalem
>   In England's green and pleasant land.''

99

This was as truly the resolve of the sons of the Oxford Movement as it is that of their socialistic grandchildren. But their Jerusalem was quite definitely a Christian Church.

Nor would it be just to them to suggest that they ignored the essential sociality of the spiritual life. The thought of the Church as the mystical Body of Christ which expresses precisely this fact in the form of a religious dogma was very familiar and significant to them, though not, perhaps, carried out to the point at which, in the devotional writings of one of the second generation of the Movement, the late Father Richard Meux Benson, founder of the Cowley Society of St. John the Evangelist, it sometimes seems even to threaten the permanence of individual personality.

Yet even when justice is done to these features of their teaching, it remains true that the men of the Oxford Movement, sons of an age in which the philosophy dominant in their country was profoundly individualistic, and in which the influence of Hegelianism had as yet not seriously affected English thought, did not keep clearly in view that essentially social character of the bestowal of grace through sacraments, by the recognition of which alone can they be satisfactorily discriminated from magical rites. And it is obvious that this discrimination becomes most important in the case of baptism because this was the only sacrament commonly administered in the Church of England to recipients unquestionably incapable of

a voluntary act of faith. Moreover, that aspect
the Oxford Movement in which, in the spirit of
the great Romantic movement, of which it was in
one point of view a part, it sought to restore to
religion and to life the mystery whereof the
rationalistic Enlightenment had seemed to empty
them, disposed it to accept without unwillingness
a doctrine so mysterious as that of the implan-
tation in the soul, by means of the administration
of baptism to the body in unconscious infancy, of
a seed of new moral and spiritual life, needing,
perhaps, to be fostered hereafter by other means,
but no less truly there from the first than is in the
embryo the potentiality of physical human life
from the moment of conception.

The insistence by the Tractarians on the doctrine of Baptismal Regeneration, plainly asserted,
it is true, in the Prayer-Book service, was closely
bound up with their whole conception of the
Christian life as a mysterious incorporation of the
individual personality into the Humanity of God
Incarnate, whereby the powers of that humanity
are imparted to it in principle and are at its dis-
posal in proportion to the absence in the individual
of the obstacle which sin puts in the way of the
free course of divine grace, and also to the positive response of faith and love with which the
individual meets the offer of that grace ; a response
which, however, must no doubt be regarded as
itself originally the effect of the presence of that
grace in the soul. At the same time their reverence

for ecclesiastical tradition and their readiness to welcome mystery in religion prevented them from stumbling at the peculiar difficulty created by the application to infant baptism of language which might pass without criticism where submission to baptism was the regular and normal expression and seal of a conversion to Christ, wherein the offer of forgiveness for sins past and thereby of justification—the declaration that the convert was cleared of guilt—was solemnly accepted by the individual of his own free will.

§ 3. THE GORHAM JUDGMENT

In 1849, the Bishop of Exeter, Henry Phill-potts, having refused to institute to a living in his diocese, on the ground that he denied the doctrine of the Church of England, a Calvinistic clergy-man named Gorham, who held that the grace of regeneration was not, strictly speaking, granted *in* baptism, but either as "prevenient grace" prior to it or afterwards at conversion. The Court of Arches upheld the Bishop in his refusal, but the Judicial Committee of the Privy Council to whom Gorham appealed decided that the views in question did not constitute a ground for such action. There was naturally great searching of hearts on this occasion in the Tractarian party, which was now led by Pusey—for Newman had seceded to Rome five years previously. There

were not a few, Keble among them, who thought
that the toleration of Gorham by a court which,
though they questioned its competence, was
de facto the supreme tribunal of the Church of
England, gravely compromised the position of
that Church as an orthodox branch of the Catholic
Church. Pusey, however, while he readily lent
the assistance of his learning in Christian antiquity
to the Bishop in preparing his defence, and
though he had been always especially prominent
as a defender of the doctrine which Gorham was
supposed to have impugned, was less moved than
many of his followers. It was characteristic that
this was in part due to his sympathy with the
jealousy of the Evangelicals for the claims of *conversion,* which he rightly held to lie behind their
dislike of language about Baptismal Regeneration which, though theologically accurate, was
genuinely misunderstood as denying the need of
conversion whenever there had been baptism in
infancy. He addressed a letter to the newspapers
in which he quoted as evidence of this the statement of Gorham's chief apologist, a certain
Goode. "The great and all-important doctrine,"
Goode had said, "to be contended for is that an
adult is not necessarily in a state of spiritual regeneration because he was baptized as an infant."
"If Mr. Goode means by this," Pusey com-
mented, "that an adult is not necessarily in a
state of grace, and so may require a solid and
entire conversion, notwithstanding the gift of God

in baptism, no Christian instructed in the first principles of the Faith would contend with him.''[1] That same fundamental emphasis on the primary importance of a good life which had inspired the Tractarian dislike of any doctrine which appeared to recommend instead of it reliance on mere feeling under the name of faith was equally at variance with any substitution for it of trust in a past reception of sacramental grace, however real that reception may have been at the time. Accordingly, after the Privy Council's judgment had been delivered, we find Pusey declaring at a meeting of High Churchmen at Freemasons' Hall in London that '' Peace will be best secured by laying down truly and in all its depth and fulness and in its connection with the Incarnation and death and merits of Christ the truth of Baptismal Regeneration, but also by laying down the other truth that those who have been made in baptism the children of God must by God's grace live as children of God, and those who have fallen from that grace must be restored by a thorough conversion to God.'' Pusey, however, although in this way ready to do justice to the motive of his opponents in the controversy, and satisfied that the Privy Council's decision had not involved the Church of England in the guilt of heresy, yet joined in protests against the judgment and declarations that he and those who thought with him would continue to teach Baptismal Regenera-

[1] Letter to the Press, December, 1849.

tion not merely as a tolerated opinion, but as the genuine doctrine of the Church.

On account of this action, one of the ablest of the Tractarians, James Mozley, Newman's brother-in-law, afterwards Regius Professor of Divinity at Oxford, having come to the conclusion that the Gorham judgment was substantially right, and that there was nothing inconsistent with the Church's teaching in denying that baptism necessarily and in every case involved regeneration, thought himself bound to dissociate himself from Pusey and his friends, and gave up his connection with the *Christian Remembrancer,* the organ of the party which they led, though continuing in sympathy with their general line of thought. In a work full of learning and good sense, in which some seven years later he reviewed the whole controversy, he pointed out that the key to it lay in the fact that the practice of infant baptism had been introduced into and maintained in the Church "in combination with the idea of an institution primarily for adults."[1] The Church had "never ventured upon the step of a total removal of the infant from the basis of the adult in baptism."[2] The fathers and the schoolmen maintained that the infant as such was qualified for the grace of baptism, since it offered no impediment to it. The divines of the Reformation, on the other hand, maintained that baptism was always condi-

[1] *The Baptismal Controversy,* p. 23.
[2] *Ibid.*

tional, and that infants and adults stood upon the same ground—namely, that of faith and repentance. There were two Reformed theories : one that baptism was in the infant's case an anticipatory rite, and was only attended by grace when its recipient as an adult believed and repented ; the other the theory of a "prevenient grace," which implanted faith in the infant before baptism. This was thought to remove the difficulty of supposing justification in baptism without faith, a difficulty which St. Thomas had met by supposing justifying faith to be given in baptism, a supposition which was, however, plainly open to the objection that faith was no longer under this scheme, as St. Paul's teaching would seem to imply, the antecedent *condition* of justification, but an integral *part* of it. Mozley's conclusion was that as "Scripture is silent with respect to infants as recipients of the grace of baptism . . . it follows that though the doctors of antiquity give one plan of this omitted ground, the doctors of the Reformation another, neither plan can, according to the rule of faith adopted by our Church, compel our acceptance, and that therefore, according to the rule of our Church, the regeneration of all infants is not an article of faith "[1] ; and this was precisely what the Gorham judgment had affirmed.

The term "regenerate" was no doubt used in the Anglican formularies of all baptized infants ;

[1] P. 226.

but the term was from Patristic times onwards
ambiguous. It had, firstly, a " poetical, rhetorical, or hypothetical " sense, carrying on the language of the Old Testament about the chosen
people, and that of the New Testament about the
Church as a whole, where the whole nation or
Church "is by supposition regarded as being
what certain individuals of it really are";
secondly, a "technical or conventional" sense,
in which it is only used as a term for outward and
visible baptism ; thirdly, a "doctrinal sense ; and
under this head we have," says Mozley, "first,
the general statement that regeneration is the
grace of baptism ; secondly, that adults are regenerate in baptism upon the condition of faith
and repentance ; and, thirdly, that all infants are
regenerate in baptism."[1] The main body of language employed in the primitive Church, down
to A.D. 300, was composed with adult baptism
specially in mind.

Ignoring the ambiguity of the ancient usage
and the special application of the earliest language to adult baptism only, Pusey, says Mozley,
while he earnestly rejects any other sense of the
word "regenerate" than the very highest, or
that implying actual goodness, yet deprecates
any less extensive application of the term than
that which includes all baptized infants. This
combination of the highest sense with the universal
application is nowhere, Mozley complains,[2] ex-

[1] P. 177.   [2] P. 175 n.

plained in the text of Pusey's Tract on the subject. The assumption that the limited and special
use of the term "regeneration" in connection
with baptism has the *precedence* above the other
higher and fuller sense, "so that the sense of
actual conversion of heart has to be apologized
for," he declares to be a departure from the older
traditions of Anglican—even of High Church
Anglican—theology.[1]

I have given at some length some of the principal positions of Mozley's treatise because it
exhibits so clearly the issues at stake in the controversy ; but I have omitted any reference to that
important part of it which deals with the problems
raised by the combination (as in St. Augustine
and in some of the Reformers) of a strongly pre-
destinarian doctrine with a belief in a connection
between regeneration and baptism ; because this
is not a combination characteristic of the
Tractarian theology, though it had a very direct
bearing on the question of Gorham's orthodoxy.
But there are two points in Mozley's treatment
to which I desire to draw special attention ; one
on account of the illustration which it affords of
what Dr. Brilioth calls the "moralism" of the
Oxford school ; the other because it exemplifies
what I have elsewhere noted as a defect of the
mode of thought which that school as a whole
shared with most of their contemporaries in this
country.

[1] P. 173.

1. On the first point I will give some significant quotations. "Is it reasonable," asks Mozley,[1] "to suppose that a moral habit can be imparted to a human being by a particular outward rite? Such a result is less startling in the case of infants because the germ and commencement of life is in itself a kind of mystery. But we must feel great difficulty in the idea of a moral habit being formed by an external rite in the grown and mature man. Such an effect of the sacrament comes into direct collision with reasonable modes of thinking of which we find ourselves possessed." Some, perhaps many, Tractarians would have stumbled at this plain-spoken statement; but the unhesitating appeal to the moral consciousness is thoroughly in accord with the main tradition of their theology. "*The* acceptable thing in the sight of God," Mozley adds,[2] "is actual holiness and goodness : where this is had, no defect of ritual can possibly interfere with the individual's favour in his sight."

2. On the second point I would remark that the whole discussion, as conducted by Mozley, proceeds upon thoroughly individualistic lines. Individual salvation occupies the central place in his thought ; the conception of the nation or Church as a spiritual unity, to which moral predicates can be applied, is, as we have seen, to him merely "poetical, rhetorical, or hypothetical," asserting of a group what is, in point of fact, only true of

[1] P. 128.　　　　　　　[2] P. 130.

certain members of it. The possibility that our pride in the achievements, our shame at the failures, of our country or our college, though we may not ourselves have contributed to them, points to a genuine social consciousness as a real feature of our human nature, never seems to occur to him. But, as we have seen, this is only a striking exhibition of a lack which characterizes Tractarian thought in general, notwithstanding the party's mission of receiving the idea of the Church as an article of Christian faith. It was necessary for the English mind to experience the influence of the Hegelian philosophy, on the one hand, and of the Darwinian biology on the other before that idea could have its full effect on the theology of the school. A strong mystical bent might in an individual teacher, as we see in the instance of Richard Meux Benson, anticipate this full effect ; but is only with the *Lux Mundi* group, who stood under both the influences I have mentioned, that the notion of the Church as a truly organic unity can be said to have established itself in Anglo-Catholic thought.

VI

TRACTARIAN MORALISM AND ITS CONSEQUENCES

§ 1. PLAN OF THE CHAPTER

I COME back, therefore, to the emphasis on obedience to the moral law as the preliminary condition of justification and an holiness as the aim of the life of him whose sins have been forgiven as the predominant characteristic of the teaching of the Oxford Movement. It remains (1) to discuss the relation of this emphasis to that laid by another school of piety on the free offer to sinners of salvation through the blood of Christ on the sole condition of faith therein ; (2) to show that the theory of faith which was worked out by Newman most fully after his secession, in his *Grammar of Assent,* but which is a real development of his earlier thought and of that implicit in the whole teaching of the Oxford Movement, is an outgrowth of the "moralism" (I use Dr. Brilioth's word, but without the slight touch of disparagement which, I think, attaches to it as he uses it), which is the central feature of Anglo-Catholic theology ; (3) to examine the bearing of this theory and of the "moralism" from which it springs on the distinction of the "natural" from the "supernatural" life which is so important in Roman Catholic teaching, and which has recently been persuasively expounded and defended by the late Baron Friedrich von Hügel; (4) to indicate one or two directions in which the ruling idea of the Oxford Movement has worked itself out in ways which would have been highly uncongenial to its original leaders, but which are accordant with the results of quite other tendencies in contemporary thought and sentiment.

§ 2. Tractarian and Evangelical Views of Justification

1. I begin with discussing the relation of the Tractarian to the Evangelical view of Justification. I am not proposing to go at length into the history of the doctrine of Justification, but rather to attempt to indicate what were the essential elements in the Tractarian view and in that to which it was directly opposed, and to indicate how they may be said to supplement each other, each laying stress on a point which the other tends to overlook.

The doctrine which the Tractarians encountered in the Evangelicalism of their day and against which they reacted was, I suppose, less that of the Reformers (though a recent work by an Irish bishop, O'Brien, had expounded the Lutheran doctrine, and was the object of Tractarian criticism) than that which had been brought into vogue by an earlier Oxford Movement—that of the Methodists. It will perhaps be, therefore, relevant to say something here of Wesley's teaching on the subject—all the more that it presents in some ways a striking resemblance to that of the Tractarians themselves, especially in respect of what Dr. Brilioth calls "moralism"—and to note where it took a different line from theirs, a line in which some of Wesley's followers went far beyond what Wesley himself ever approved.

Unquestionably, Wesley began his career very much as the Tractarians did, urging on a generation suspicious of everything in religion which savoured of what they called (using the word as one of disparagement) "enthusiasm," the Christian duty of aspiring after a holiness beyond any within the reach of human nature unassisted by supernatural grace. "The circumcision of the heart," he told his hearers at St. Mary's in a University sermon preached in 1733, just a hundred years before that Assize Sermon of Keble's, the day of the delivery of which Newman regarded as the "birthday of the Oxford Movement"—"the circumcision of the heart is that habitual disposition of soul which, in the sacred writings, is termed 'holiness'; and which directly implies the being cleansed from sin, from all filthiness of flesh and spirit; and by consequence the being endued with those virtues which were also in Christ Jesus ; the being so re-newed in the image of our mind as to be perfect as our Father in heaven is perfect." Here we have (remarks his biographer, Tyerman[1]) propounded in the plainest terms, as early as the year 1733, Wesley's famous doctrine of Christian perfection. "This sermon," said he, in 1765, "contained all that I now teach concerning salvation from all sin and loving God with an undivided heart."

Not only was Wesley's teaching, like that of the Tractarians, inspired by this passionate desire for holiness, but it also, like theirs, emphasized the acceptableness of moral obedience, even when not accompanied by mature Christian faith. As late as 1780 he wrote : "What is the faith which is properly saving ? It is such a divine conviction of God and the things of God as even in its infant state enables everyone that possesses it to fear God and so work righteousness. And whosoever in every nation believes thus far is accepted of Him. He actually is at that very moment in a state of acceptance. But he is at present only a *servant* of God, not properly a *son*. Meanwhile be it well observed that the wrath of God no longer abideth on him."[2]

But the religious experience of Wesley differed in an important respect from that of the Trac-tarians. What he reckoned as his " conversion "

[1] Quoted by Tyerman, *Life of Wesley,* i., p. 88.
[2] Tyerman, i., p. 167.

took place in 1738 under the influence of the Moravian, Peter Böhler, when he was thirty-five years old and had been ten years in Holy Orders. Nor had he, up to that time, been without serious impressions of religion ; he had been, on the contrary, for a long while the leader of a religious movement which had from the first been of a definitely "High Church" character, laying especial stress upon the importance of the sacraments of the Gospel. Newman's conversion had occurred when he was a boy of fifteen ; it lay behind him when he came to hold high sacramental doctrine, and it could be interpreted as an arousing within his soul of the grace implanted in baptism, even although its source in the mystical union effected by the sacrament was not realized until long afterwards. In Wesley the conviction that he had suddenly become possessed of a faith which he had hitherto lacked, the assurance of his justification thereby, created the consciousness of being born again and made a new creature. He would seem, indeed, never to have abandoned his belief that infants are regenerated in baptism ; for he expressly observes[1] that persons who are baptized when adults are not always simultaneously born again, apparently distinguishing them in this respect from infants ; and, as we have already seen in the case of Pusey, there is no necessary inconsistency between faith in baptismal regeneration and a belief that a real conversion of the

[1] Tyerman, i., p. 230.

Evangelical type more often than not is necessary even to the baptized. But unquestionably the practical emphasis is, with Wesley, wholly on conversion, and whatever his theory of its relation to the bestowal of regenerating grace in baptism may have been, in Methodism the latter was completely overshadowed by the former, and the difference between Tractarianism and Evangelicalism of the Wesleyan type consists in the disconnection in the latter of justification from the sacraments and the greatly increased importance attached to the individual's *feeling* as the test of its reality.

There lies at the bottom of the controversy here involved a difficulty which is familiar in other departments of speculation than that which relates to religious experience. It is the difficulty created by the facts (1) that our ultimate evidence of the reality of anything must in every case be a direct experience or consciousness either of that thing or of something with the existence of which it is necessarily connected, and (2) that no such direct consciousness of an object which may occur to any one of us can be taken at its face value, or is exempt from the possibility of illusion and error. It will be sufficient to illustrate this universally present difficulty from the case of our consciousness of other persons, the case to which our consciousness of God presents the closest analogy. I am convinced that without a direct consciousness of being in *rapport,* so to say, with another person—without, that is to say, an experience of actual social intercourse—we could not arrive at the conviction of the existence of other persons by an inference from any experience of a different sort in which there is not already presupposed the reality of such experience, though not necessarily the fact, of *this* experience being such. Yet no independent criterion can be assigned whereby an individual's conviction that he here and now is dealing with another real person can be finally and certainly discriminated from an illusion. The criterion most commonly used is, of course, confirmation by the experience of *others*; but, even putting aside the consideration that for any particular individual his belief in the existence of these others themselves is in principle equally open to doubt, we have to reckon with the possibility of collective hallucination on the one hand, and with the possibility on the other (no doubt one less readily conceded, but not unthinkable) of personal communication by means or under conditions which one's neighbours could not by the ordinary use of their senses detect.

In the present case, therefore, the strong point of what we may for the moment call the Evangelical view lies in its appeal to direct experience, which must always be the ultimate court of appeal. The belief that I have been forgiven or justified in baptism, or because I am intellectually convinced of the truth of certain doctrines, may be what the Tractarians themselves were in the habit of calling a "merely notional" belief, but one carrying with it that feeling of being immediately in contact with the object, comparable to the experience of sense-perception, which at the moment seems to exclude all doubt. Such a belief might seem to be a "real" belief in contrast with a merely "notional" one. The Evangelical demands this kind of belief, and, where it is found, accepts it without demur. Nor can the follower of the school opposed to his deny that *such* a direct consciousness, if attainable and when genuine, would—other things being equal—surpass in value any conviction to which such a direct consciousness was lacking. For though there may be a higher moral value in the faith of him who "has not seen but yet has believed"[1] than in that of one who needs sight before he believes at all, yet the beatific vision is commonly regarded as the goal of faith, and this must certainly be held to involve a direct consciousness of the object expressible by the word "vision" borrowed from sense-perception. Yet a very little attention to the history of Evangelical piety shows how peculiarly liable to fluctuation and uncertainty is the test of feeling. We see this in Wesley's own experience. "Many hundreds in London," he says in 1770, "were made partakers of [Christian perfection] within sixteen or eighteen months, but I doubt whether twenty of them are now as holy and as happy as they were."[2] This being "made par-

[1] John xx. 29. [2] Tyerman, iii., p. 59.

takers of Christian perfection'' meant an assurance of sanctification similar to the assurance of justification connected with the conversion which the same persons had experienced at an earlier stage of their spiritual career. Wesley believed that this assurance was granted to some. But he was continually having to contend against the danger of neglecting obedience to the moral law as superfluous. Though he held that a man ought not to believe that he is fully sanctified till he has '' the testimony of the Spirit witnessing his entire sanctification as clearly as his justification,'' yet he declares that all ought to wait for this great change, ''not in careless indifference or indolent inactivity,'' but '' in vigorous universal obedience, in a zealous keeping of all the Commandments, as well as in earnest prayer and fasting and in close attendance on all the ordinances of God.'' '' If any man,'' he says, '' dreams of attaining it in any other way, yea, or of keeping it when attained, he deceiveth his own soul. It is true we receive it by simple faith ; but God does not, will not, give that faith unless we seek it with all diligence in the way which he hath ordained.''[1]

Although he owed to the ministry of a Moravian preacher, Peter Böhler, what he reckoned to be his own definite conversion, he was utterly repelled from Moravianism by the doctrine, current among Moravians, of a sanctification

[1] *Ibid.*, ii., p. 347.

instantaneously and simultaneously attained along with justification by faith alone, and completely divorced from obedience and self-denial. When Count Zinzendorf, the founder of modern Moravianism, said to him[1] that "all Christian perfection is wholly imputed, not inherent," that "our whole justification and sanctification are in the same instant—from the moment anyone is justified, the heart is as pure as it ever will be"— Wesley asked : "Do we not, while we deny ourselves, die more and more to the world and live to God?" Zinzendorf's reply was : "We reject all self-denial. We trample upon it. We do, as believers, whatever we will, and nothing more. We laugh at all mortification. No purification precedes perfect love." No wonder Wesley came to warn his followers against Moravianism, "the most refined antinomianism," as he calls it, "that ever was under the sun,"[2] "producing the grossest libertinism, the most flagrant breach of every moral precept." But he needed to warn them. His own teaching is often very near to that of the Tractarians ; but the point in which he differed from them, his belief in an assurance given by feeling for which we ought to look, was the seed of a tendency in his societies in the direction, if not of antinomianism, at least of under-valuing the importance of moral conduct and of personal humility, a tendency against

[1] Tyerman, i., p. 339.
[2] *Ibid.*, iii., p. 467.

which he was continually struggling. Those who think they have attained are to speak (he tells them) of their own experience with great wariness, and with the deepest humility and self-abasement before God. Young preachers are not to speak of perfection in public "too minutely or circumstantially, but rather in general and scriptural terms."[1] It was in contrast with the reliance on the test of feeling, with its obvious dangers, that the Tractarians fell back upon the objective fact of baptism ; in contrast with a facile assurance of having attained Christian perfection, on a recommendation of a perpetual penitence, which shrank, above all things, from abandoning itself to the emotional enjoyment of the possession of that real holiness which they, as strongly as the Methodists themselves, held to be the proper consequence of the impartation of Christ's Spirit, not the mere imputation of his merits, to the members of his mystical body.

In truth, the Christian life must continually exhibit—indeed, it may be said to consist in—a tension between the factors mutually opposite, but equally indispensable to the fulness of a religious experience of the Christian type. That there is (as it has been put) no unpardoned penitent, that genuine repentance suffices to call forth the divine forgiveness, apart from anything over and above repentance, required, like a legal formality, to give effect to an act of will already

[1] Tyerman, ii., p. 307.

complete—this conviction, which is the inner meaning of the doctrine of Justification by faith alone, and on which it is the peculiar mission of Evangelicalism to insist, is not really inconsistent with the recognition of the absolute obligation of the moral law, which, indeed, is presupposed by the very penitence which secures this immediate pardon. But it may lead to its being forgotten, just as conversely the stern judgment of sin which such recognition may engender may lead us, with the elder brother in the Parable of the Prodigal Son, to a complacent sense of superiority to the open sinner, which, in fact, implies in him who indulges it an inadequate appreciation of the exactingness of that very demand of the moral law itself upon the conscience, the sense of which supplies a seeming justification to his attitude. So again we find one man who, in his preoccupation with the traditional means and conditions of attaining to holiness (or what the Methodists called Christian perfection), misses that joy and peace in believing which others simply accept when it comes to them as substantial participation in the Holy Spirit ; and we find another who, taking a mere feeling of assurance in abstraction from the particular acts in which a holy life expresses itself for such substantial participation, misses the security which no feeling, exposed as it must be to vicissitudes due to physical and psychical changes, can afford. But at the root of the apparently opposite errors of both these lies an inadequate appreciation of what would correspond to the idea of that very holiness, the passion for which is the ruling motive of either.

§ 3. NEWMAN'S DOCTRINE OF FAITH

2. My next remarks will concern the doctrine of faith which, as worked out by Newman, eventually took shape, after his submission to Rome, in the *Grammar of Assent,* but which is an undoubted product of the Oxford Movement. It is, however, also, as we find it expounded by Newman, stamped with the peculiar seal of his individual genius. So far as it emphasizes religious faith as rooted in the moral consciousness, it is true to the strong ethical bent which is the outstanding characteristic of the whole Movement; and it illustrates the side of Tractarian doctrine which recalls the teaching of Kant, who also associated faith with the practical or moral as distinguished from the theoretical or scientific Reason. So far as it tends to lay stress on the thought implicit in mental processes largely carried on (in more modern language) below the threshold of consciousness and to a great extent determined by individual experiences and associations rather than on the explicit reasoning which offers itself to dispassionate public criticism, it is profoundly characteristic of Newman's idiosyncrasy.

In his *Lectures on Romanism,* delivered in 1838, seven years before he left the Church of England, we find him telling us[1] that Faith differs from opinion in its considering God's "being, governance, and will as a matter of personal interest and importance to us, not the degree of light or darkness in which it perceives the truth concerning them." In the following year, preaching before the University of Oxford on "Faith and Sight," he constantly contrasts the *personal* character of religious Faith with the nature of Reason as ignoring or abstracting from personal differences. "As we reprobate," he says, "under the name of Utilitarianism the substitution of Reason for Conscience, so perchance it is a parallel error to teach that a process of Reason is a *sine qua non* for true religious Faith."[2] On this ground he turns away from the "evidences" which had occupied so much of the attention of English theologians for a century—precisely because their appeal was made equally to all men independently of their diversity in respect of moral character and religious experience. They might be "of great service to persons in particular frames of mind"[3]; they might startle the careless, test honesty of mind, encourage perplexed believers; but, after all, the kind of proof alleged by the evidential writers—*e.g.,* from

---

[1] P. 106.
[2] *University Sermons,* p. 175.
[3] P. 191.

ERRATA

Page 124, line 9: *For* "Faith and Sight," *read* "Faith and Reason contrasted as Habits of Mind."

Page 125, line 5: *For* "Faith and Reason," *read* "The Nature of Faith in relation to Reason."

ERRATA

miracles, "is," he observes, "a sort of proof which a man does not make for himself." There is in it "nothing inward, nothing personal. There is no room for choice." In another University Sermon preached in the same year on "Faith and Reason," he will not have Faith made to depend and follow on a distinct act of Reason beforehand. "The act of Faith is sole and elementary and complete in itself, depends on no process of mind previous to it."[1] "Faith is the reasoning of a religious mind," which feels the Gospel message to be probable, "because he has a love for it, his love being strong, though the testimony is weak."[2] It is indeed "an act of Reason," "but of what the world would call weak, bad, or insufficient Reason; and that because it rests on presumption more and on evidence less."[3] "The diversity with which men reason"[4] on the same facts, in all departments, and not only on religion shows us that Faith is not the only exercise of Reason which approves itself to some and not to others, or is, in the common sense of the word, irrational. Reason seems sometimes to be identified with explicit reasoning; but often it is extended to cover more than this. Thus, we read, men "may argue badly, but they reason well—that is, their professed grounds are no sufficient measure of their real ones—and in like manner, though the evidence with which Faith is content

[1] P. 194.   [2] P. 195.
[3] P. 196.   [4] P. 202.

is apparently inadequate to its purpose, yet this is no proof of real weakness or imperfection in its reasoning."[1] "As Reason with its great conclusions is confessedly a higher instrument than Sense with its secure premises, so Faith rises above Reason in its subject matter more than it falls below it in the obscurity of its process."[2] "Faith is a process of the Reason in which so much of the grounds of inference cannot be exhibited, so much lies in the character of the mind itself" (that is, of course, of the *individual* mind, not of the mind *überhaupt,* as Kant would put it), "in its general view of things . . . that it will ever seem to the world irrational and despicable—that is, till the event confirms it."[3] "The act of mind by which an unlearned person savingly believes the Gospel may be analogous to the exercise of sagacity in a great statesman or general, supernatural grace doing for the uncultivated reason what genius does for them."[4] "As far as its being a test of moral character is of the essence of religious Faith, so far its being an antecedent judgment or presumption is of its essence."[5] "Some safeguard of Faith," it is admitted, "is needed which will secure it from becoming superstition or fanaticism."[6] But this safeguard cannot be Reason ; the exhortations to cultivate the reason, give education, and the like, which were then the cry of the Liberals, whom

---

[1] P. 205.   [2] P. 208.   [3] P. 210.
[4] P. 211.   [5] P. 223.   [6] P. 226.

Newman regarded as his chief opponents, over-looked the very point on which he, with the Tractarians in general, was most concerned to insist—namely, the *moral* presuppositions of religious knowledge. "The safeguard of Faith," he declares, "is a right state of heart. It is holiness or dutifulness, or the new creation of the spiritual mind. It is love ; or, in scholastic language, justifying Faith, whether in Pagan, Jew, or Christian is *fides formata charitate*."[1] This last remark, aimed as it doubtless is at the Lutheran doctrine that the faith which justifies is *fides informis,* shows that in his doctrine of Faith Newman is fighting, so to say, on two fronts as a champion of morality. Religion is for him never a matter of faith *alone,* or of reason *alone.* "Ultra Protestants" and Liberals, with all their differences, agree in ignoring the absolute necessity of moral conduct as the primary pre-requisite of true religion.

But we must distinguish from this insistence on the moral elements in religious faith, in which, of course, Newman is on the same side with Kant, another feature, characteristic of Newman's view, and in his own mind closely connected with the moral character of faith, but one in which there is an obvious difference, at any rate, at first sight, between his account and Kant's ; I mean his insistence on the *personal* character of faith, as distinct from the *impersonal* character

[1] P. 228.

of reason. I have elsewhere[1] discussed Kant's view of the relation of *personality* to *reason;* and this is not the place to go into it, as not Kant but Newman is our subject at present. But unquestionably, from Newman's point of view, and using Newman's language, Kant may fairly be said to have laid stress on the *impersonal* nature of morality, in the sense that he thought of the goodwill as essentially abstracting from individual differences and willing that which was law universal for all rational beings. To Newman, on the other hand, morality and religion with it belonged precisely to that sphere of individual personal experience in which one's whole self was involved, and which could be on that very account contrasted with the purely rational or scientific speculation in which abstraction is made of all individual and personal characteristics, of all the circumstances of one's individual and personal history, and only that is taken into account which is the same for all men capable of recognizing the cogency of logical and mathematical reasoning. Moreover, this *personal* character of religious faith was connected with the fact that it is only by means of faith that we recognize the *personality* of God. "Natural religion," he says,[2] "teaches the infinite power of majesty, the wisdom and goodness, the moral goverance, and in one sense

[1] In my Gifford Lectures on *God and Personality,* p. 117 f.
[2] *University Sermons,* p. 23.

the unity of the Deity; but it gives us little or no information respecting what may be called His *Personality.*" "The philosopher aspires towards a divine *principle,* the Christian towards a divine *Agent.*"[1] "The marks of design in the creation are beautiful and interesting to the believers in a God; but where men have not already recognized *God's* voice within them, ineffective, and this, moreover, possibly from some unsoundness in the intellectual basis of the argument."[2] This last remark is especially interesting because it harmonizes so closely with Kant's contention that the purely rational proofs of God's existence are actually fallacious in themselves, and that only a moral proof can, in fact, carry conviction. Newman's language, just quoted, indeed, is not free from ambiguity in so far as it sometimes seems to allow a certain perception of God's moral attributes to reason apart from the experience of conscience. He does not seem to have asked himself whether without that experience he could have perceived so much. But as usual he is preoccupied with the contrast between the *personal* character of religious faith and the *impersonal* character of the scientific reason; and it is no doubt true that, although without *some* measure of the experience of conscience, the attribution to anything of *moral* predicates could have no meaning for us, and the thought of divine *goodness* could not arise in our minds, yet so small a measure of

[1] *University Sermons,* p. 29.   [2] *Ibid,* p. 55.

this experience is sufficient that it seems negligible in comparison of the rich and profound moral experience out of which religious faith takes its rise. But some measure there must be, and it would, I think, now be generally admitted—more generally than in Newman's day—that even the attitude of mind implied in calling the supreme principle of order by the name of *God* is really justified only by a religious experience. Such an experience lies, in fact, behind the whole development of philosophical thought ; Philosophy is the daughter of Religion, even though she sometimes becomes its adversary ; but it has only been very gradually that Philosophy has come to realize this and to perceive that it must either claim to have so outgrown that experience that it can express all of reality that was communicated to the mind therein in a non-religious form, or allow that there are aspects of reality which are not apprehended so long as no account is taken of such definitely religious experience as the old rational theology tended to ignore.

Newman's theory of development in theology anticipated in a very real sense the movement of thought which was soon to change the whole face of English philosophy, when, the discoveries of Darwin having suggested a *modus operandi,* the notion of evolution or development, which had already appeared as a grand philosophical principle in the system of Hegel (then little studied or understood in this country), took its place as a ruling idea in every department of thought. And in the same way his theory, announced in the *Grammar of Assent,* of the "illative sense," "the personal action of the ratiocinative faculty," puts us in mind of the old notion of a logical inference as a quasi-mechanical process of syllogistic deduction from premises, which could be adequately carried on by such an actual machine as the ingenuity of Jevons devised, and the substitution, therefore, of a view which recognizes in it a living activity of the mind. "The reasoning faculty, as exercised by gifted or by educated or otherwise well-prepared minds, has its function in the beginning, middle, and end of all verbal discussion and inquiry, and in every step of the process. It is a rule to itself, and appeals to no judgment beyond its own."[1] So Newman describes the "illative sense," and modern logicians would agree with him that such was the nature of the faculty whereby we draw conclusions from the facts before us, but would hesitate to follow him when he goes on to say that this "illative sense supplies no common measure between mind and mind," and that it is "nothing else than a personal gift or acquisition."[2]

It is, of course, a question of much interest and great difficulty that Newman's doctrine of the illative sense raises. Every act of inference is the act of some thinker, and forms, as such, part of a whole which is individual and unique. On the

[1] *Grammar of Assent,* p. 361.   [2] *Ibid.,* p. 362.

other hand, in respect of its logical character as a
conclusion from premises, it forms part of another
whole, which we call a chain or system of reasoning. There seem, indeed, to be two different and
disparate principles which unify our experience.
There is, as I have elsewhere said, "one which
combines premises with the conclusions which
follow from them, the thought of causes with the
thought of their effects, the members of series
with what comes next to them in mathematical or
logical order. It distinguishes logical priority
from temporal, mere sequence from necessary
connection, one kind of subject or department of
knowledge from another, and so forth, though one
may, so to say, through greater or less vigour of
mind, or more or less abundant opportunity, be
able to make more or less use of it than his
fellows. . . . The other principle combines and
disjoins experiences on quite a different plan. It
combines all sensations, perceptions, thoughts
which I call *mine* together as *mine,* no matter how
little logical or generally intelligible connection
they have with one another. It divides all sensations, perceptions, thoughts of *yours* from all of
mine, no matter how closely they resemble mine.
If by communication through speech or writing
or otherwise, my thoughts are conveyed to you or
yours to me, they must be reckoned twice over,
as yours and as mine, although their content be
identical."[1]

[1] *God and Personality,* p. 114.

It is not hard in this way to distinguish these two principles, but it is very hard to frame a satisfactory account of their mutual relations. In what we call the exact sciences, the personal or individual factor seems to be least important. The personal equation is treated as something to be discounted or allowed for as a possible source of error ; but in what we reckon as the highest regions of thought, in poetry, religion, philosophy, it seems impossible to abstract the thought from the personality of the thinker, as is done in the exact sciences. Hence we cannot study the results reached by the thought of great poets, prophets, or philosophers, apart from their original setting, as we can with those reached by great men of science.[1] But what concerns us chiefly at present is the fact that Newman's interest was principally in what we may call the *personal* principle of unity in our thinking ; and here, too, his teaching reflected his own experience. Some people do reach their convictions by ways of which a great part is not explicitly in consciousness, while others reach them by processes of reasoning and argument of all the steps of which they are well aware. Newman belonged to the former class ; and his phrase ''the illative sense'' commemorates this fact. We may, indeed, agree with him that '' there is no ultimate

---

[1] See my paper on '' The Personal Element in Philosophy '' in the *Proceedings of the Aristotelian Society* for 1905.

test of truth besides the testimony borne to truth by the mind itself,"[1] but may yet allow that it belongs to the very essence of the mind itself, though it is always an individual mind — to transcend its own individuality by recognizing in itself something genuinely common to it with all other minds, the apprehension of a common object, the use of a common instrument, nay, more a nature which is truly one in the diversity of the persons whose nature it is.

We shall not, I think, find in Newman a satisfactory treatment of the whole question ; but we shall find a striking presentation of the *personal* factor in the thinking of us all, and we shall note that his main concern in discussing the subject is with its bearing on his fundamental conviction that religious conclusions are determined rather by moral character than by purely theoretical reasoning : and his main interest in it closely bound up with that intense preoccupation with his own inward history which placed him among the great autobiographers. This preoccupation is, of course, all his own ; but the conviction I mentioned above is characteristic of the whole Oxford Movement.

§ 4. NATURAL AND SUPERNATURAL

3. There are few more interesting or difficult questions in religious ethics than that suggested

[1] *Grammar of Assent,* p. 350.

by the contrast of *natural* and *supernatural* in the sphere of conduct. In what I am now going to say, I shall constantly refer to the address of the late Baron von Hügel on *Christianity and the Supernatural*.[1]

The theory defended in this address is that of the legitimacy of recognizing *two levels* of moral life ; both of them required for the full exhibition of the ideal, so that the exclusion of either impoverishes the ideal itself, and in some degree spoils the factor which remains. I have dwelt already in the first chapter of this book on that aspect of the Reformation of the sixteenth century, in which it appeared as a movement for the rejection, in the interest of a genuine Evangelical Christianity, of any dualism in the moral standard, and as thus involving the disappearance of those monastic institutions which had embodied the older recognition of *counsels of perfection* for a few by the side of *precepts* addressed to all. I need not, therefore, now repeat what I have said, but will merely ask my readers to bear it now in mind. It was admitted that there was loss as well as gain in this disappearance ; that with special temptations to hypocrisy there went also special aids to sanctity, and with an improvement of standard consequent

---

[1] Originally delivered in Oxford in 1920, and printed in his *Essays and Addresses on the Philosophy of Religion,* Series I., pp. 278 ff. : with which should be taken one or two paragraphs of another paper on pp. 223-4 of the same book.

on the cessation of certain practices, by which the support of the organizations intended to facilitate a stricter devotion was made to compensate for laxity in their supporters, a lowering of the aim of devout aspiration and a subordination of religious demands to the exigencies of secular life.

Thus in one aspect the denial of the legitimacy of recognizing *two levels* of achievement may be criticized as tending to result in a *lowering of the general* level, through the disappearance of any provision for what was regarded as a higher than that to which the generality of men can be expected to attain. In another, however, it may be criticized as requiring of *all,* and so as making *necessary* to goodness in every case such a conscious and deliberate mortification of natural affections as under a "two-level" system was only demanded of those who set out to follow the "counsels of perfection" and renounce the world altogether. Defenders of the "two-level" theory therefore point to the contrast between a theology which, looking in all Christians for something like the religious experience depicted in the epistles of St. Paul, neglects the lesson taught by such passages in the Gospels as those which describe our Lord's welcome of little children as, in their simplicity, what we should call their lack of self-consciousness, the very type of what the citizen of the kingdom of heaven should be ; or, again, to the contrast between the insistence on love as the fulfilling of the law and the Kantian suspicion (in which Kant was a true son of the Protestant Reformation) of duties done with liking, as most probably not done from the truly moral motive at all. I do not know that any definite defence of the doctrine of "two levels" is to be found in the writers of the Oxford Movement ; though I am by no means prepared to assert that one could not be found ; but I feel fairly certain that we cannot call the doctrine as stated—*e.g.,* by von Hügel—a tenet of the Tractarian school. At the same time the sympathy of the school would certainly have been with its defenders in both the points that I have just mentioned. The admiration of the fairer side, at any rate, of monasticism is characteristic of the Tractarians, and although the refusal by them and by the great majority of their successors to demand celibacy from the clergy generally has been, and is to the last degree, important as a security against any real Romanization of the Church of England, the successful restoration under Anglo-Catholic influence[1] of monastic institutions alike for men and women within the Church of England is a significant result of their principles and an immediate consequence of the Oxford men's reluctance to share the current Protestant suspicion of any cultivation of holiness which shall involve a withdrawal from the ordinary activities of the householder and citizen. So much

[1] I use the word Anglo-Catholic in its wide sense, as including the Tractarians and their more moderate as well as their extremer followers.

for the first ground on which a one-level theory is criticized by the champions of a two-level theory. As to the second ground, we have already seen that Tractarian theology was characterized by a frank recognition of the genuine value of obedience to the moral law, apart from the acknowledgment of definitely Christian or even explicitly religious sanctions ; also that it inherited from the older High Churchmen the defence of natural piety against a Puritan rigorism in which Hooker had engaged in his controversy with Cartwright ; and we may here further note a fact to which Dean Church has rightly called attention in his well-known book on the Oxford Movement, that it was part of its mission to go back from an Evangelicalism which identified the *Gospel* with the scheme of redemption elaborated in the Pauline Epistles to an emphasis upon the primacy for Christians of the *Gospels* and the record therein of the teaching of Jesus himself, which could claim the sanction of the Catholic tradition embodied in the ceremonial honours accorded in the ancient Liturgies to the public reading of that portion of the Scriptures above that of any other.

The contrast of Nature and Supernature raises a great many questions of the deepest interest and importance. A full discussion of it would lead us to inquire into the relation between the confession that when we have done all that we are commanded we are still but "unprofitable servants" and the view that we cannot do *more*

than our duty, except in the merely legal and
external sense in which our duty means that which
other men can demand of us under penalty. It
would examine the significance of the admiration
we feel for what we are inclined to call the moral
genius of a Socrates or the religious genius of a
Francis, an admiration which may seem quite
different from our approval of the moral excellence
which we sometimes suppose to be exhibited
equally by everyone who does his best, no matter
in how humble a sphere ; since we no more think
it within the capacity of everyone to be a Socrates
or a Francis than we think it within the capacity
of everyone to be a Shakespeare or a Beethoven.
It would investigate the claim of the Church to
mediate a higher level of spiritual life than the
State *can* mediate, a claim which philosophers of
the Hegelian school, such as the late Mr. Bosan-
quet would explicitly deny. But as the men of the
Oxford Movement do not, as far as I know,
advance a formal doctrine of two levels, it is not
necessary to follow out that doctrine into its
furthest consequences. We may, however, I
think, say that they were in sympathy rather with
the Catholic type of doctrine, to which the doctrine of the " two levels " belongs, than with the
opposite, or Protestant, type ; in so far as this
means, on the one side, a ready appreciation of
such goodness as children may display, into
which neither the strenuousness of moral effort
nor the religious consciousness of sin has entered ;

on the other, an aspiration after a kind of holiness which so far transcends the utmost demands of any society primarily designed for the satisfaction of man's natural (including his intellectual) needs that it requires for its cultivation by human beings a distinct society of supernatural origin, a new Jerusalem "descending out of heaven from God."

It is interesting to contrast Tractarianism here, not with the Evangelical Protestantism to which we have hitherto most often opposed it, but with the position of one whose religion was no less predominantly ethical than theirs, yet was, perhaps, of all their opponents the one whose hostility was the most implacable, just because it was based, not so much on prejudice as on a profound difference of outlook, of which he was fully conscious. I mean Thomas Arnold, the famous Headmaster of Rugby, who branded them as "the Oxford Malignants." There is an interesting story in a letter of Newman, describing his last and almost his only meeting with Arnold in 1842, a few months before Arnold's death, when Arnold was dining with Provost Hawkins at an Oriel gaudy, and Newman, as Senior Fellow, was in the chair in Common-room. "Baden Powell made some irreverent remark, and people were amused to see how both Arnold and myself in different ways, as far as manner was concerned, retired from it."[1] There was in both Arnold and

---

[1] *Letters and Correspondence,* ii., p. 442.

Newman a profound seriousness to which anything irreverent would have been at once repellent.
We have already remarked upon the passage of
Ward from discipleship to Arnold to discipleship
to Newman, to each of which masters he was
drawn by their *ethical* teaching, but of whom he
came to prefer Newman to Arnold, because
Arnold seemed to him to have stopped short
where Newman went further. This "stopping
short," as eventually it seemed to Ward to be,
consisted in precisely the absence from Arnold's
teaching of the emphasis which Newman and the
Tractarians laid upon aspiration after a holiness
for which the duties of secular life were inadequate to afford sufficient scope, and which must
thus necessarily seek expression in such systematic asceticism and such devotion to prayer
and worship of a larger measure of time than is
compatible with the duties of secular life as involved the revival of institutions of the kind which
had ministered to similar aspirations in the whole
Western Church before the Reformation and in
the Roman Catholic part of it since. And this
absence from Arnold's Churchmanship of an
element to be found in Newman's was, as will
easily be perceived, closely connected with the
former's attachment to an ideal which the older
Anglican High Churchmen, from their great
master, Hooker, onward, had especially cherished,
of the identification in a Christian country of
Church and State. Under the circumstances of a

later age the realization of this ideal was clearly, to say the least, very much more difficult than the men of the sixteenth and seventeenth centuries could be expected to recognize ; and perhaps few theories of the period we are now considering seem to us now more impracticable and fantastic than the deliberate return of Arnold, under Coleridge's inspiration, to the platform of men who lived when the admission of non-Christians to full citizenship, and the toleration of all religious opinions which do not practically outrage public morals, was still unthought of. To the end Arnold wished to exclude Jews from full citizenship, while desiring to expand the national Church so as to include all Christians. Many who would have been reckoned as his allies against the Tractarians did not share his peculiar view on this point—his German friend, the Chevalier Bunsen, for instance, and Archbishop Whately, from whom, indeed, Newman considered that he himself had first learned his conception of the Church as a distinct and independent society. But Arnold's view of the Church was logically connected with precisely that deficiency in his teaching which Ward felt when comparing him with Newman. No doubt Arnold himself would not have allowed that it implied a "stopping short" in ethical aspiration. To him it seemed that the effort to distinguish the Church, as a society, from the *Christian* State was to lower the standard of the latter below the standard of the Gospel : and this he held to be unworthy of a society consisting of professing Christians. And, in fact, this must be the consequence of a definite abandonment, such as we find any modern European State committed to, even though in different degrees of completeness corresponding to the extent to which in the various nations the Christian tradition has maintained its hold upon the people, of any attempt to enforce upon the whole community the Christian law as such. But Arnold's identification of the Church with the Christian State certainly carried with it, on the other hand, an assumption that certain ways of life which the general tradition of the Church, down to the time of the Reformation at least, had regarded with approval and even reverence, were not characteristic of Christianity at all, but rather opposed to its spirit ; for from the nature of the case they implied a certain withdrawal from the ordinary duties of citizenship on the ground of a religious call of higher urgency than the political community's demand that they should be fulfilled. No doubt, as in the case of military service, to which a monastic vocation has often been compared, the State may itself (the remark is, of course, St. Paul's[1]) call some of its members to free themselves from entanglement with the affairs of ordinary civil life, for a purpose of its own, but then the purpose *is* its own ; the purpose of the monastic or similar religious vocation is

[1] 2 Tim. ii. 4.

"other-worldly," and could only be adopted by the State if the State committed itself to a general view incompatible with, according to secularists and other non-Christians, equal citizenship with Christians. Although, as we have seen, the Tractarians did not adopt a formal doctrine of two levels, they were unquestionably bound to part company with anyone who, like Arnold, was prepared to identify the Church, as the society whose life is the Christian ideal, with any Christian State which could possibly live in the modern world. Yet they would not have been at all prepared to abandon any claim on the part of Christianity to influence political and secular life, or to treat baptized persons as other than by right full members of the Church. Thus they were certainly more in sympathy with the position of those who definitely recognize "two levels" than with that of men like Arnold, whose opposition to such a recognition determined their whole theory of conduct. But it would probably be an error to attribute to them as a school a uniform and consistent doctrine on the subject, which is, indeed, one of great difficulty, and the thorough-going consideration of which would take beyond the limits, not only of my present subject, but of the sphere within which I am conscious of having reached assured conclusions. I will therefore leave this topic with two observations :

1. I do not think that the Christian conscience can approve the recognition of a double standard

for an individual Christian on an individual occasion. If he is really called to exceptional self-denial, it is his *duty* to respond to the call, and he sins if he fails to respond. This is none the less true because, just for the very reason that the self-denial *is* exceptional, no one *else* has the right to treat him as an open sinner or a criminal because he so fails, if he does not fall below the standard of self-denial which is accepted as generally required of members of the community. I say "the community," using this term vaguely. For plainly a man would be rightly regarded with disapproval in a circle of professing Christians who was known to be indulging himself in vices or allowing himself opportunities of pecuniary profit which in a different circle would be so common as not to incur reprobation.

2. The second point which I wish to make is this : The admission of exceptional calls for special sacrifices from individual Christians does not involve the assumption that particular modes of life which happen to imply forbearance from gratifying certain desires which are strong in the generality of human beings are of necessity on that account higher and more meritorious in themselves than modes of life in which the absence of something precious to the majority of human beings is not so patent. The most obvious instance of which is, in my mind, of course, the instance of *celibacy*. The Gospel recognizes[1] for

---

[1] Matt. xix. 12.

those who "are able to receive the saying" the value of the self-denial of those who "make themselves eunuchs for the kingdom of heaven's sake." Voluntary celibacy for a religious motive may, no doubt, exist apart from any monastic institutions, but there is no question that the existence of such institutions facilitates such voluntary celibacy, and enables those who feel themselves called thereto to respond to the call at once more easily and more effectively, since it implies the recognition of it as a possible mode of service and the provision of definite tasks for those who undertake it. Where such institutions exist they will be quite justifiably used by persons in whom voluntary celibacy involves no particular heroism, and who would have remained single in any case; but it is clear that those who fall under this description have no claim whatever to be regarded as living a higher life than that of the married citizen, many of whose trials and opportunities of service they, as a matter of fact, escape. No one can suppose that the enormously high proportion of celibates among the saints canonized by the Roman Church represents even remotely the actual distribution of heroic self-denial between those who marry and those who do not. This exaltation of celibacy as such is a feature of Catholic tradition, against which Protestantism in general has strongly reacted; for the Oxford Movement it had a certain fascination, and it must, I think, be allowed that the complete disappearance of monastic institutions from the Churches of the Reformation was a real loss, whatever the medieval abuses which precipitated it. The Tractarians and their successors, in restoring to the Anglican Church a real opportunity for those who have a vocation to the celibate life to fulfil it to the best advantage by the foundation, first, of numerous sisterhoods, which have fully justified their existence, and afterwards by that of such brotherhoods as those whose headquarters are at Cowley and at Mirfield, while at the same time there has never been any really serious movement among them to confine the priesthood to celibates, may, perhaps, be said to have shown a rare appreciation in this matter of the true *via media* between extremes which have both alike been found disastrous to the maintenance of the true balance of that genuine Christian morality which finds room at once for the hallowing of the normal life of the many, and for the world-renouncing enthusiasm of the few.

I should like here to call attention to a paragraph of the essay by the late Baron von Hügel, to which I have already referred, on *Christianity and the Supernatural*,[1] in which he doubtless speaks as a Roman Catholic with a certain tenderness for the usages of his own communion, but in which, while claiming a high place for religious celibacy in the life of the Christian Church, he recognizes very candidly "the beneficence of a

[1] *Essays and Addresses*, pp. 285-7.

married clergy" and the "dangers and draw-backs of too large an extension of obligatory celibacy."

§ 5. LATER DEVELOPMENTS OF TRACTARIANISM

4. The last of the four topics on which I pro-posed to touch was the fact that in certain direc-tions that emphasis on morality which I have attempted to show was the dominant idea of the Oxford Movement worked itself into directions which would not have approved themselves to the leaders of that Movement. In entering upon this subject, I wish to make clear that I do not attri-bute to the Anglo-Catholic school the initiative in the changes of theological view to which I shall call attention ; I only contend that the principles of that school prevented it from effectively resist-ing the tendency to these changes.

The first change is one of immense importance. I mean the change of attitude towards the Bible which results from the free critical study of it. Of the three historical schools of thought within the Church of England, it was, as one would expect, the so-called Broad Church school which was the pioneer here. Jowett's essay in *Essays and Reviews* on "The Interpretation of Scripture" was already in advance of Mr. (now Bishop) Gore's celebrated contribution to *Lux Mundi* on "The Holy Spirit and Inspiration." The influence of the Oxford Movement had no doubt weakened to some extent the emphasis on the " Bible and the Bible only " as "the religion of Protestants," which was characteristic of the Evangelicals by placing beside it as its authorized interpreter the tradition of the Fathers of the Church, and by recognizing the Church as the primary teacher of Christian truth, rather than Scripture, whose special function was to prove what the Church had taught. But the Tractarians had held a doctrine of the inspiration of Scripture in no degree less high than that of the " Evangelicals," and this predilection for the system of "mystical interpretation," which they found recommended to them by patristic and medieval authority, rather encouraged than otherwise in them the conviction that every word of Holy Writ had its own lesson or lessons to teach us, if we can but find it out. It was half a century after the original Oxford Movement that one who afterwards came to be esteemed the most distinguished divine of the school which reckoned itself the successor of the Tractarians, and who already, as head of the Pusey House, held a position which identified him with their tradition, led the younger generation of his party (to the dismay of many in the elder) frankly to recognize the established results of Old Testament criticism and to give up, in consequence, the belief that critical questions could be held as prejudiced by the references of Jesus to David as the author of a psalm or to Daniel as that of the predictions which went under his name, and so to allow that our Lord's knowledge was limited in certain directions.

The strong ethical bent which we have observed to be characteristic of the school was well illustrated in this revolution in its doctrine. It was his strong sense of the *duty* of intellectual honesty which mainly impelled Charles Gore to break with tradition in this respect, and if in the school of which he is an ornament many have since gone much further than he in this direction, if the whole attitude to the Bible has changed within as without that school from what it was forty years ago in all schools that reckoned themselves orthodox, it is, I think, unquestionable that the traditional Tractarian insistence on the value of common morality as the necessary presupposition of religious experience has assisted in making the change possible and even inevitable for men who felt themselves, notwithstanding, to be faithful to the fundamental principles of the religious movement to which they were attached.

The other change in attitude to which I shall refer is that in respect of the doctrine of eternal punishment. Here again the Tractarians are certainly not to be credited with the initiative. They were entirely in agreement with all the orthodox schools in affirming this doctrine. We find Newman saying in his "Lectures on Romanism" that "there can be no instance among ourselves of sincere Christians being tempted, as Origen was,

to question what is meant by the eternal punishment destined for the finally impenitent." The
remark illustrates how little the men of that
generation anticipated the change which was to
come over the temper of the whole Church in this
regard—in this country, at any rate—within
three-quarters of a century;[1] a change which is
by no means to be felt only where the doctrine in
question would be in set times denied. We are
now only concerned with the part played by the
theology of the Oxford Movement in leading to
this change. It was, I think, very closely
analogous to that which it played in bringing
about the change which we have already discussed, in the attitude of theological teachers
towards the Bible. Here, too, there was certainly
no intention on the part of the Tractarian teachers
to innovate on the common doctrine of all schools
who professed orthodoxy. But, just as the
Tractarians by refusing to isolate the authority of
the Bible, as was done by those whom they called
"ultra-Protestants," and by reincorporating it,
so to say, in the general authority of the Church,
whose Book it was and from whom we received it,
undoubtedly tended to *subordinate* that authority
in the minds of their adherents and in that way to
prepare them for the far greater change which the

---

[1] By 1870 Newman had become aware that the belief
in eternal punishment was " dying out in all classes of
our own society." Vide *Grammar of Assent,* Pt. II.,
c. x., § 2, 9 (ed. 1891, pp. 459, 460).

progress of criticism was to entail; so, too, while not consciously differing from the Evangelicals in their eschatology, yet by refusing to isolate the doctrine of the Atonement as though it were the sole essential content of the Gospel message—and by reincorporating it in the doctrine of the Incarnation and laying the main stress of their teaching upon the mystical union of the Christian with Christ which was effected through the sacraments rather than upon the forensic imputation of his merits consequent upon the mere act of faith, the Tractarians tended to *subordinate* in the minds of their adherents the aspect of the Gospel message on which what is sometimes called the "hell-fire preaching" of another school had almost exclusively dwelt. But, just as in the case of the authority of the Bible, so, too, here, this alteration of emphasis, while it no doubt prepared the way for the acceptance of a far more drastic change, did so without any intention of the kind on the part of the divines of the Oxford school. The initiative in that change in the Church of England came from quite other quarters, as the names of Frederick Denison Maurice and of Frederick Farrar suggest, but the effects of it are now, of course, apparent in the school which inherits the Tractarian tradition as well. And here again the motive which has brought the men of this school to sympathize with doubts to which their predecessors would not have confessed is their loyalty to the great Tractarian principle that the religious experience is rooted in the moral and that no doctrine which is really felt to be irreconcilable with conscience can be a genuine part of true religion.

In conclusion, I am very conscious of the very imperfect treatment which I have given to a subject of real historical interest and also of the absence of novelty from my main contention that what Dr. Brilioth calls "moralism" is the ruling idea of the religious philosophy of the Oxford Movement. But I think those who will acquaint themselves further with the literature and history of the Movement will find that this *is* the ruling idea of that philosophy in the light of which the detailed developments of it are best understood. It was the conviction of the Tractarians (*a*) that the religious experience is rooted in the moral, and (*b*) that the genuine development of religious experience involves an aspiration after moral perfection or holiness.

In their controversy with the two schools of theology with which they were contemporary and from which they were concerned to dissociate themselves, it was the former aspect of their general emphasis on ethics that determined their opposition to the Evangelicals, the latter that determined their opposition to the Liberals. As against the Evangelicals they may be said to have assisted the immanence of the religious values in the whole ethical development of humanity ; as against the Liberals, the transcendence by those values of the national order as represented by secular civilization. They stood for a religion neither merely "revealed" nor merely "natural," but for one in which Revelation carried on to higher issues the work of that indwelling Conscience to which it necessarily first addressed itself and which it could never be interested in gainsaying.

INDEX

INDEX

PRINTED IN GREAT BRITAIN BY
BILLING AND SONS, LTD., GUILDFORD AND ESHER